Ellen Hodges Cooley

The Boom of a Western City

Ellen Hodges Cooley

The Boom of a Western City

ISBN/EAN: 9783743309067

Manufactured in Europe, USA, Canada, Australia, Japa

Cover: Foto ©ninafisch / pixelio.de

Manufactured and distributed by brebook publishing software (www.brebook.com)

Ellen Hodges Cooley

The Boom of a Western City

THE HEARTHSTONE SERIES

A series of GOOD STORIES in an attractive form at a low price

50 cents each

A QUESTION OF DAMAGES	J. T. Trowbridge
THE CAMPION DIAMONDS	Sophie May
THE MAN WHO STOLE A MEETING HOUSE	J. T. Trowbridge
GETTING AN INDORSER	By Oliver Optic (William T. Adams)
THE BOOM OF A WESTERN CITY	Ellen J. Cooley
EXILED FROM TWO LANDS	Everett T. Tomlinson

Our Complete Catalogue sent on application

LEE and SHEPARD Publishers Boston

THE

BOOM OF A WESTERN CITY

BY

ELLEN HODGES COOLEY

"*Its birth a deed obstetric without peer;
Its growth a source of wonder far and near.*"

BOSTON
LEE AND SHEPARD PUBLISHERS
10 MILK STREET
1897

TYPOGRAPHY BY C. J. PETERS & SON, BOSTON.

PRESSWORK BY BERWICK & SMITH.

CONTENTS

PART		PAGE
I.	A Step in the Scale of Gradation	1
II.	The Fulness of Life	19
III.	Regression	70

PREFACE

I WAS for some years a resident of the city about which I write, and have held strictly to the spirit that pervades a new Western town. My description of its mode of conducting business, and of its society at that time, is hardly an exaggeration; while many of the incidents were of actual occurrence, though given under fictitious names and such change of circumstance that there can be no complaint of personal allusion.

E. H. C.

the well-being of his race, he is also answerable for inventing diseases resistless and contagious.

In the spring of 1878, the United States Mail brought to Blankridge, through papers and letters, a species of fever of human invention, — the Western fever. Many were smitten. Schoolboys speedily recovered, but under its influence several of the surplus professional men departed their unpatronized Eastern life. Of the "ne'er-do-wells," fortune favored one only with a new start, and he reached the goal indirectly. An inferior position on a railroad that ran between Blankridge and Montreal was offered him. It proved a stepping-stone to roads west, and finally landed him in Fargo, Dakota, while the city was very young, though ripe for its "boom."

Unknown to his neighbors, the disease attacked one of the most reliable and respected citizens of the town, — Jonathan Bullard, resident of acres that three previous generations of his lineage had held in possession. In harmony with the operations of Nature, and after the temperament of its victim, it wrought slowly and silently, but none the less surely.

In March it knew throes; gusty inclinations to a sudden decision, — a state which Mr. Bullard's judgment termed desperate, — followed by spaces of calm. In April confidence and doubt contended, as sunshine and showers. May brought calm. His mind brooded, as the sun broods over earth's embryos. Through June, July, and August his purpose grew, and with the ripened harvest was matured. He now disclosed his mental condition to his family; and Almira, the only daughter, felt herself inoculated. The subject entered into daily conversation; and as all the other members save Mira had escaped infection, scenes followed the nearest resembling family jars that had ever occurred in this hitherto united household. Mr. Bullard wished to dispose of his farm, and take the proceeds, with his family, to Fargo.

"What's the use of grubbing along here year in and year out, as father and grandfather did," he argued, "and, after all, when you die leave nothing but the same old meadows, the same old sprout-land, and the same old hills?"

"Heighty-tighty!" cried grandmother. "Jonathan thinks the Lord is goin' to give him power to create new land out West!"

"No, I don't, Grannie. What I think is, that the Lord has a land which 'floweth with milk and honey' waiting for us; and if we do not go up and take it, we shall be rebels just as much as the children of Israel were when they refused Canaan."

Almira ran for the family Bible, and fortified her father's position by reading selections from the thirteenth and fourteenth chapters of Numbers. When she paused, Jonathan junior, a sturdy lad of fourteen, made comment: "I wa'n't born in Egypt; I live in Blankridge. Too many miles and too many years stand between that story and me. We don't think it 'plies; do we, Grannie?"

After the death of Grandfather Bullard, the boy's belongings had been transferred to his grandmother's cottage on a farm adjoining his father's; and he knew himself to be already practical proprietor there, while legal transfer only awaited his majority. He was loyal to the trust, and walked in Grannie's paths, and swore by her decisions, regardless of other ties.

Poor Mrs. Bullard, the wife, confessed to a "perfect flutter" of indecision; but this mental state was of such frequent occurrence on all subjects, that it received little sympathy from the family, and weakened her influence on either side of the question. Regard and duty pleaded in favor of her husband and daughter; inclination and "sense" bound her to Grannie and her son. Thus rent, her suspended decision ran : —

"I wish we'd never seen the newspapers; then 'twould have all gone on just the same. And no matter if we don't make money. Jonnie is provided for, and we've got enough ahead now to give Mira a good setting out; not that there's any particular need, for the Peterses have all got money in the bank, and to spare — if she only would."

This connection of surname and pronoun implied a desired connection, through the bond of wedlock, between Alonzo Peters and her daughter Almira. Alonzo had never, by vocal expression, given her a right to cherish such a hope; but if there is truth in the time-honored maxim, "Actions speak louder than words," he was only waiting sufficient encouragement from the lady in question to justify his giving voice to the aspiration.

Though little respected in Blankridge community, the "ne'er-do-well," Mr. Mateson, had fed the flame of Mr. Bullard's fever. By his advice the editors of the two Fargo papers, opposed in politics, had for some months supplied Blankridge village store with their daily publications; and Mrs. Mateson's letters to her friends portrayed the city as a very Eldorado. Grannie warned her son against placing confidence in newspaper items or advertisements, much less to trust the stories of "those shiftless Matesons." Mr. Bullard admitted the liability of the former to exaggeration; but had not the Mateson head sent substantial tokens of his own prosperity? And when such as he could liquidate debts that his creditors had months before crossed from the debit side of their account as less in value than the paper they covered would be to the ragman; and when, in addition, he could send cash to reclothe his family, and pay their passage to join him, did it not prove the fatness of the land neither a myth nor a hoax?

Mira had heard of these letters; and after "out West" had assumed a personal interest, she resolved to read them with her own eyes, and weigh them with her own judgment. They were easily found, and readily given for her perusal. Mrs. Mateson's description of the style of dress prevalent in Fargo was all gossip had promised; it far exceeded anything worn in their village, even by the merchant's and lawyer's wives. Interesting as was this feature of society, it impressed the present reader less than did the description of the city, — its energy, its "push," whether in amusements or improvements; its whole-souled generosity, that bound its citizens together as brethren, and had no cold shoulder for a stranger.

While this testimony was only hearsay, Mira had felt the whole current of her being setting Dakotaward; in the light of this incontestable evidence, she professed herself "just crazy to go." Mrs. Bullard listened to the story until her restless heart found haven in her daughter's enthusiasm, and her husband's convictions pinioned it there. Weary of stemming the current, Grannie next gave reluctant consent; and Jonnie thereafter held his peace.

As male head of both households, Mr. Bullard's power was supreme, and his obligation to consult the preferences or prejudices of his family could, according to the patriarchal standard in vogue in Blankridge, hardly be called a moral bond; but his youth had been carefully trained after Solomon's injunction, and his age doubly fulfilled the prophecy; for he could no more depart from his mother's positive commands than from the virtues she had inculcated.

In process of time, Mr. Bullard freely spoke of his intentions in the village; and while family objections still held his purpose in abeyance, though Blankridge was no growing town, customers came to price the property; for the reputation of the Bullard farm was as untarnished as was the character of its proprietor. "Not but what Natur' has made its ekul frequent," was decreed in the self-constituted court that held consecutive evening sittings round the village grocer's stove; "but we know jest where to find his land. His fences, they're kept up. His mow pieces ain't run out for want o' dressin'. He don't expect the ground to hold out yielding sixty bushels o' corn to an acre without a little encouragement. In consequence, his farm is worth more money to-day than it was thirty years ago; and he's made a good livin' out of it, too, and laid up money to boot, we bet."

Waiting within scorching radius of this same stove for one dollar's worth of sugar to be weighed and packaged, Alonzo Peters first heard of Mr. Bullard's proposed movement. His face assumed the hue of the glowing sheet-iron that had generously responded to the full draft turned on by a customer who came in chilly from a long ride; then it paled so wofully as to attract attention, even in the imperfect light diffused through the smoky chimneys of kerosene burners.

"Sick, Lon?" asked a friend. "You look as white as a sheet."

"I do feel a little faintish. Getting too warm, I guess;" and he pushed his chair behind the molasses hogshead, thus screening himself not only from the miniature fiery furnace, but from the lamp's disclosures and his friend's gaze.

"Sugar's ready," called the grocer. But it was some moments before the young man could summon fortitude to rise, or find strength to bear his purchase forth.

Though Alonzo's respect for the Bullard family was sincere, only one member of it was capable of hastening or retarding his pulse; only one woman in the world was capable of reducing his strong manhood to the weakness above recorded. Outside, the keen November blast was inadequate to nerve his feeble pulse; but it did brace his timid heart to the extent of resolving to seek Almira Bullard that very night, and tell her, not his hopes, for these had vanished before the great destiny that awaited her, but his love, his fears.

Absorbed in this intention, he passed his father's door, oblivious of his package until its lessening weight awoke him to the consciousness that he was literally making sweet his path with its contents. Retracing his steps, he dropped the despoiled purchase on the kitchen table, hoping to escape unseen.

"What has happened, Alonzo?" cried his mother, entering from the sitting-room just as he was in the act of escaping through the outer entrance. "Have you been robbed?" spying his flabby parcel.

Ignoring the saccharine loss in the supreme loss approaching, Alonzo's reply, borne back on the breeze occasioned by his rapid exit, was in accordance with his thought, —

"Going to be!"

Mrs. Peters sank into a chair, too bewildered to take the comfort that peaceful times afforded from the knowledge that the sitting-room china-closet contained a gun; or to gather inspiring confidence from the fact that her husband was even then sitting with his chair tipped back against the door of this same recess, his head reposing on its centre panel.

Weather prophets had said the sky betokened snow; and as Alonzo rapidly made his way toward Mr. Bullard's house, their prediction was spitefully fulfilled.

"More likely to find her home, and less likely to find company," he muttered, drawing down the earlaps of his cap, and tucking his coat-sleeves into the long wristers of his home-knit mittens. Light streamed cheerily from their parlor windows. It fortified his courage, if it did not inspire hope. Jonnie responded to his knock.

"Come in; we are all here talking it over," was his pleasant greeting.

Alonzo was in no mood to "talk it over" in family assembly, but he could find no excuse for not entering. He was greeted not only by both branches of the Bullard family, but Patience Armstrong, the "fashionable dressmaker" of Blankridge, sat with her feet on the fender, looking so domesticated that he felt sure any attempt to see Mira alone that evening, or probably for a week to come, would prove futile. But he was mistaken in his inference that

Miss Armstrong was a permanent guest: for no sooner had he risen to depart, as the clock struck nine, than she jumped up, declaring that she, too, must go; and as their road lay in the same direction, he had no choice but to escort her, not only as far as his own door, but to her own, a good mile beyond.

Not until he had left Miss Armstrong under the protection of her father's roof, refusing her urgent invitation to enter in language more terse than courteous, did Alonzo have opportunity to cherish his disappointment in not having been able to see Almira alone, or to reflect upon the further light that the evening's conversation had thrown upon the family flitting. Almira had told him that she anticipated the proposed change with unmingled delight, that she had used all her influence to win her mother's consent, and that she should leave Blankridge without one sigh of regret. Mr. Bullard had fully discussed his prospects of selling out, named the price he set on his farm, and said he hoped to dispose of the livestock and household effects just as they stood. When the conversation became animated, and so general that there was no danger of her being overheard, Mrs. Bullard had drawn him aside, and confided many of her vacillations to him: for he was on very friendly terms with the mother; indeed, more at ease with her than with the daughter.

He thought of the subject all the way home. It lay uppermost in his mind while apologizing to his mother for his hasty manner of the early evening. It flooded his brain all through the long watches of the night. Irritating as had been the necessity of accompanying Miss Armstrong home, his sacrifice had brought its reward. She had told him that a day would intervene before commencing her reign at Mr. Bullard's. "And then I shall most likely be there up to the very last, they are both having so much," she explained.

"But the farm isn't disposed of yet. I thought their going was contingent upon that?" Alonzo made this assertion a query, in order to further draw out his companion.

"There are three different parties ready to take it to-morrow, live-stock and all," she answered. "But they don't want the furniture. He won't hold off long on account of that, though, for 'twould fetch more at auction; and that he allows, only he has taken a whim to lump the whole thing. I tell him 'tis a leading that he'll come back in the spring, and want it all again; and I only wish I had the cash to buy him out. Wouldn't I make him pay well for his little holiday! I'd make as much as I can save in ten years at my trade."

Tossing and turning wearily on his bed, his whole sentient being enveloped in darkness more obscure than the rayless night, suddenly a meteor light flashed across Alonzo's mental vision. Why should not he make the purchase — possess himself of the whole

Bullard estate? His own bank-book would go far toward payment, and his father's would meet the balance. His mother had often urged his setting up for himself; and though the connubial partnership she advocated with Miss Armstrong was little to his taste, time would disabuse her of that illusion.

To till her father's acres, to milk his cows, to guide his oxen, to drive his horse, would be a close link between himself and Mira. To dwell in the rooms she had glorified with her presence would, albeit melancholy, be consolation triumphant for his loss. He would hold everything as in trust; for they might return, as Patience had suggested. Then he would relinquish his claim, and win at least her gratitude. Alonzo had not been educated in florid speech, and he thought this out in very commonplace idiom. Yet none the less was his heart as full of devotion as is the poet's, and of passion as is the poet's song.

At the breakfast-table he stated his desire to purchase the Bullard estate, and the proposal met with no opposition.

"The price is stiff," said Father Peters; "but there's one thing in its favor, there'll be no leakages to stop. Everything is ship-shape to begin with. You'll know just as well what land to let lay, and what to till, as though you'd owned it fifty years."

"And the house and furniture are plenty good enough for Patience Armstrong, nice as she is," cried Mrs. Peters. "I don't see anything to hinder your getting married right away."

"Pooh, pooh, mother! 'Tisn't a wife I'm looking for; 'tis a home."

" And what's a home without a wife, I should like to know? 'Tis a house without a candle, a heaven without a moon." The good woman paused, red-faced at her own eloquence. Presently, recovering herself, she continued, —

"That isn't the way you've been brought up, Alonzo, to go against women-folks."

"I don't go against you, mother. You shall be head of the house; and I'll get some strong, likely Irish girl for you to boss."

"Your father didn't begin that way. Times have changed for the worse." Mrs. Peters emphasized this assertion with a sigh.

"After the chores are done up, I think I'll go over and talk with Mr. Bullard this very morning," was Alonzo's response.

Mr. Peters gazed at his son in blank astonishment.

"Why, Lon! Why! What's come over you? Where's the hurry? We'll work round to it before spring ploughing comes on. Moderation and discreetion go hand in hand, my boy."

"But somebody will get ahead of us. I hear he is going to square up right away."

"I know Jonathan Bullard. He isn't the man to rush. It would look unbecoming on both sides; as if we were trying to take advantage of each other, you know."

Alonzo had every incentive to observe the proprieties, but influences were equally strong in favor of action. For the next hour torturous thought moistened his brow far more copiously than did the labor demanded by the chores. It would not let him rest; so, in spite of his father's advice, after the home claims of the morning were satisfied, he repaired to his chamber, and presently appeared before his mother dressed in his best suit of clothes.

"I guess I'll just drop over to the Bullards'," he explained. "Don't know as I shall say anything."

"You look more as if you's going to bargain for a wife than for a farm," was her response. "You'd better take in the Armstrongs' on your way home. Nobody can say you've been in a hurry there."

The little flush that greeted this advice encouraged Mrs. Peters to hope he contemplated obeying her suggestion. Unduly eager as Alonzo's parents thought him to possess the Bullard property, to possess their daughter was the source, the very fountain-head, of his desire. Consequently, arrived at their house, he first asked for Mira.

"She's gone to the barn to hunt hens' nests," said Mrs. Bullard. "Father had to go to the Centre on business, and we're going to cook up to-day, getting ready for Patience, who comes to-morrow for a long job; and Mira must help all she can. I must say, tearing up is awful, if it does have some pleasant things about it. If Mira hadn't gone in for it so strong, I could have stopped father; but I couldn't influence her. I don't know whether anybody else could."

With the young man's inquiry for her daughter, Mrs. Bullard felt her Western inclinations weaken. His visit seemed portentous. It might be capable of holding better things than even Fargo could offer. She was a modest woman, and to thrust Mira upon any one was far from her desire. But she felt there is a time for all things, and Alonzo's attentions in the past had been sufficiently marked to justify her in giving him a hint.

"Perhaps I had better go out to the barn and help her," was his response. "Climbing is dangerous for girls sometimes."

"Thank you; do," encouraged Mrs. Bullard.

He arrived at the barn too late to be of any service in Mira's quest; but their seclusion was propitious for disclosing his desire: so with the courage of honest sincerity he told his love. His suit was rejected. Indeed, Mira's whole being, heart and soul, was already so far West, that the present held hardly more significance to her than it does to a somnambulist.

"We'll always be good friends, Lon," she said when he had ceased speaking. "But I've got lots to think about now, and lots to do. Maybe if I settle in Dakota, you'll come out and visit me." Her eyes rested on his face with an expression that proved she grasped nothing nearer home than the territory she mentioned, though merriment sparkled in their depths as she continued, "They say, you know, when one jumps off the cars in those new towns, the question isn't, 'Have a hack?' 'Have a hack?' but, 'Have a husband?' 'Have a husband?' Oh, it must be great fun!"

"Perhaps you'd do just as well to take a husband nearer home," said Lon doggedly.

"Oh, 'tisn't that! I was joking. What do I want of a husband? 'Tis the life, the stir, the fun, I long for!"

"I shall never marry any one else," was his parting declaration.

Mira laughed gayly. "And I don't expect to; but let's make no rash promises."

Alonzo had hardly gained the road when he met Mr. Bullard returning home. They exchanged greetings. The younger man felt himself possessed by the spirit of acquisitiveness. It was that which spoke, and not his father's caution.

"I am thinking of buying your farm, Mr. Bullard."

"Well done, Lon! It's just the thing for you! Strange I never thought of it, for I've heard your father say a dozen times he wished you'd set up for yourself. I've put the price low, but I'll be hanged if I wouldn't come down a peg or two to you."

Alonzo would not accept the invitation to "come in and talk it over;" but he followed Mr. Bullard to the barn, assisted in removing the harness from the horse, discussing the animal's merits meanwhile, counted the cattle, commended the goodly store of fodder, inquired the breed of fowl, and even admired the cats. And he then and there resolved to bind Mira to him to the extent of immediate purchase. Though to possess himself of her accidents was a poor substitute for herself, it would at least savor of spiritual association.

To Father Peters's confusion of intellect, the writings of transfer were drawn in less than a month, signed, sealed, and recorded. The purchase included all the household stores; not an article was disturbed. Personal wardrobe alone was removed.

"Such a thing was never heard of in the country as jumping into so much so sudden," Mr. Peters repeatedly declared. "I am afraid it won't hold good. Such hurry isn't natural. It is *on*-natural. I can't think what's come over Jonathan Bullard."

His puzzled condition was somewhat relieved by Mr. Bullard's confession that "it most put him out of breath to do things up in such a hurry."

Could Mr. Peters have known his wife's secret wish, he would have thought her "possessed." She hoped the wheel of fortune would not pause in its swift revolutions until it had united her son, through the holy bond of matrimony, to Blankridge's fashionable dressmaker, Patience Armstrong.

The former proprietor did not impede the wheel's impetus by long continuance in the house Alonzo had purchased. On the evening of the twenty-sixth of December the express-train paused at Blankridge Station; and Jonathan Bullard, his wife and daughter, were the passengers for whom it was signalled. An unprecedented crowd gathered to see them off.

"Dear Lon, don't look so sober!" whispered Mira, as they stood apart. "You know I have always loved you, from my very babyhood. We shall meet again; every fibre of my being tells me so."

Her sincerity was none the less genuine that the artlessness of girlhood marked it. But her tone was light; for the solemnity appropriate to so wide a separation, into "foreign parts" as Crannie termed their removal, was crowded out by exultation.

PART II

THE FULNESS OF LIFE

The Northern Pacific Railroad employed Western men on its trains. They alone were fitted to endure the rigors of the climate, they alone were suited to the pressing demands of a new country. Their zeal, their energy, their "push," were indispensable to cope with Nature's formations, — her mighty rivers, her boundless prairies. Such was the theoretic decree of the powers that ruled.

In fact, the employees were restless, reckless characters from north, south, and east, whose elastic consciences allowed them to make false oaths respecting their own lineage, or on any other subject that pleased their fancy or seemed to advance their interests.

On the last day of December, 1878, the through train from the East found itself losing time when about one hundred miles west of Minneapolis. The wind was dead against it; and if the clouds were not dispensing snow, the elements were getting up a decided "blizzard" with that already fallen.

As though connected by a magnetic battery, the breast of every train-hand, from the highest official to the ignoble chore-boy, felt himself animated by the contest with Nature. The engineer replenished his fire. "Worth the risk!" he mentally cried, remembering his boiler lacked the strength of youth, or the flexibility of modern invention. As nearly as was possible for an obese person, devoid of literal or spiritual wings, the conductor flew from carriage to carriage. Impatient of the demands due to the smaller way-stations, the person in charge of the brakes applied them too soon, discovered he was stopping the train a half-mile outside the settlement, then whizzed them on again. Before mechanical combination could accommodate itself to such rapid changes, they were equally far beyond the station. It was all the same. Passengers were *qui vive*. Men passed and repassed, doubled and redoubled, with a rapidity that puzzled even their dogs, who fastened themselves on the wrong masters, then, in olfactory disgust, fled in rabid haste. Like the tumblers in a circus, boys were under everybody's feet, and under the car-wheels, too, for aught anybody knew or cared. A few women shrieked, and a few of Eastern origin would have fainted had there been time for "nonsense." This programme was repeated, with slight variations, at every stopping-place until they reached Moorehead. Time-tables indicated that our train and that on the Manitoba road should meet at this city; but emulation was the motto of each engineer, and the departing whistle of the latter engine sounded triumphantly as the former drew up to the station. Chagrin added its stamp to the countenances that had before blazed with enthusiasm, — chagrin, that assumed the hue of literal mortification when the telegraph operator rushed out to inform the conductor that he was beaten by eight seconds; when the station agent called to the engineer, "Reckon you took a nap on the road!" when the restaurant waiters chaffed the porters for sluggishness, and the station bootblacks the train ditto.

The cars were more than crowded; they were packed, they were jammed. It was as if all creation had awakened to Horace Greeley's advice, "Go West, young man! Go West!" Whatever the temperature outside, inside the carriages the heat was intense. "Nothing stingy about Western men. Pile in the wood!" The most sluggish blood on board was fired. It reciprocated the engineer's mental ejaculation, "I'll come in ahead at Fargo, if my old filibuster," indicating his engine, "lands us in hell!" In just fifty-nine and three-sevenths seconds the train was again in motion, only nine and one-seventh seconds behind the departure of the Manitoba. Passengers crowded out of the cars on to the platforms and steps. Eager faces from within tried in vain to peer through the frost-encrusted windows. All sentient being was *en rapport* with the race, though night shadows and the blinding snow would have cheated vision had the roads run parallel. To accomplish the short mile between the station left behind and Fargo was the task of a moment — a breath, a puff! Yet again was enginery unequal to the occasion. It shot past the Headquarters (hotel and station-house combined) as though propelled by powder. Every official knew that the Western train was due at Fargo simultaneously with their own arrival; that the double track extended only about three furlongs beyond the station; that the switch would be turned to accommodate the down train; that a miracle could not stop them within those three furlongs unless magic remodelled their whole machinery, and that double-distilled magic could not accomplish this in the time allotted, nor even think it out. Yet not a heart quaked, not a cheek blanched. Their blood mounted to the height of rapture.

"Hooray! Something will turn up! We never yet got *left!*"

The switchman was literally Western and alert.

Whiz-z-z! He spied the flying headlight while it was yet on the bridge between the two cities; took in that the Western train was not in sight. One dash at the switch — O. K.! He sprang back in season not to be drawn under by suction. One more successful stroke; no time for trial skill. Whiz-z-z! Back flew the reversed engine, obedient to the no less skilful control of its master; and in its wake the down lightning express followed close, yet not so close but the last wheel of the last coach on the Eastern train was safe on its own track, and the switch righted to accommodate its legitimate transfer.

"'Scaped by a hair's breadth!" chuckled the switchman, he alone fully cognizant of the sublime feat. Of course his hair stood on end, but that condition had become chronic. The situation was not exceptional.

Before they reached Moorehead, Mrs. Bullard had paled under the cumulation of electricity; but Mira's cheeks glowed, and her pulse kept pace with the car's progress.

"Isn't this *living!*" she cried.

"Seems to me we are hurrying up considerable," replied Mr. Bullard.

With his jackknife he scraped the frost from a portion of the window; then, making a tunnel of his hands, he pressed them close against the cleared space, and peered out. "No, we are stop" — the present participle with which intention would have concluded this sentence, by force of circumstance was changed to the past — "ed."

Before he had fairly grasped the situation, Mira cried, "Here we go again! We get off at the next station. Don't you remember? Only the Red River separates Moorehead from Fargo."

Mrs. Bullard joined in the task of collecting valises, packages, baskets, and wraps; and before they were fairly in order and apportioned to individual care, the train, after its wild chase up the road, and its backing down, all unguessed by the passengers, with a few last inane advances and recedings halted at the right spot, and our friends struggled to the platform. The contest was brief. That crowd did not consist of dawdlers. Hackmen, baggage-men, station-men, porters, clerks, boys, dogs, — all did their duty in vociferations. The engines did not subside speedily, but continued to ring and puff and whiz in the liveliest manner. Still propelled by the impetus of his surroundings, Mr. Bullard shortly found himself at the hotel office.

"Too late! Full! Try the Continental! Sixty-three ahead of you turned off!"

He looked around in hopeless bewilderment.

"Hotel on Broadway," explained a kind-hearted man, whose physical angles in the press were, without volition on his part, making fearful inroads on the flesh of all with whom unfortunate circumstance brought him in contact. "Hurry up, or everything'll be gone!"

From the entrance door Almira saw, heard, acted. She led the way, and not an instant too soon. Our party were the last pitched into the last coach. Crack went the whip; gallop went the horses; round went the wheels. Passengers were bumped and tumbled into *some* position, in which those who first entered had no advantage, for extremities mingled, as in warfare.

The Scripture promise, "The last shall be first," was fulfilled in earthly circumstance. Vying with the wind, which was driving the snow before it at the rate of a mile a minute, our driver outstripped his hurrying competitors, and drew up at the Continental entrance just in season to bar the spot from the first coach arrived from the Manitoba road. Mr. Bullard had awakened.

He was only the fifteenth man at the office, and succeeded in engaging one room, "first-class," and a cot for himself in the public hall. While asking that acceptance of these accommodations might wait upon inspection, the crowd of eager applicants had carried him, unconsciously, across the waiting-room, and half-way up the stairs; and he woke to the knowledge that, like a stump-speaker, he was preferring his request at random. In the haven of the parlors there was a lull, at least of service, though the press of occupants gave little opportunity to restore one's mental balance or right one's dress. The porters were active, and in time our party's turn came. They were ushered into a room seven feet by nine in dimensions, without a closet, without a hook, without a nail even, from which to hang a garment; while the bed, bureau, washstand, and stove, all handsome, save the latter, and all of generous size, crowded out the possibility of any chairs save one. The stove was red-hot; and a pile of pine slabs, waiting induction within its cavern, smoked from sympathy or close proximity. Mira led the way, and mounted the bed, in order to make room for her parents' ingress.

"Had calculated to put the cot up here," said Mr. Bullard; "but guess I won't try it."

"We shall *have* to have our trunks," cried Mrs. Bullard, glancing doubtfully around.

"Porter says 'tis no use to think of it to-night," her husband replied. "They can't be got at, though I gave him a quarter. Hadn't we better go to supper?"

Mr. Bullard changed places with his daughter. The ladies shook out their draperies as best they could, "fixed" their crimps, gave another shake in the hall, where there was more space, for the cots were as yet stacked against the wall, and descended the stairs. Their passage led through one end of the office, and the throng there caused Mira to remark that she was glad they hadn't put off coming another day. Her father echoed the sentiment, in his mind convinced that, had they done so, the city would not have contained them.

The table was bountifully supplied with hot biscuit, meats of every variety, and canned fruit of every description, while tall silver-plated baskets held sugared cake that promised more than it performed. But that was slight disappointment, for Dakota ozone required food more fortifying than "sweets."

Though mother and daughter took turns throughout the night in transferring generous portions of the woodpile to the stove, morning found the water in their ewer frozen. But Vermont winters were not always balmy; and after a few moments' coaxing, the stove again sent forth the glow of meridian.

When Mira threw up their window, the sun shone with dazzling splendor; the air was motionless. "A lovely springlike day," she cried. "Let's hurry through breakfast, and go out. Do have the trunks sent up while we are at the table." This last sentence was addressed to her father, who waited in the open doorway. "Oh, dear! Where *can* they go. We *must* have a larger room!" she added.

The ladies passed to the dining-room. Mr. Bullard stopped at the office. He found the clerk affable, the landlord most affable. Would be glad to accommodate with enlarged quarters, but utterly impossible. Every inch taken. Why, those who came in later thankfully piled five into a room less spacious than his. Things not quite so lively now as a month ago. Winter setting in. Business depression. Going to stay long? Never let a room to one party for over a week. Unfair to transients. Oh, yes; trunks should be sent up at earliest ability. Good deal of a jam of baggage. If theirs should happen to be at the bottom of a pile, might have to wait two or three days. But rest easy; things'll be pushed. "We are not the kind of people that hang back. 'Git!' is our motto. Rather different from the East."

Mr. Bullard was shown the accumulation of baggage. It was formidable; some of it was in the hall, much piled on the sidewalk beside the outer door. His own was not visible.

"Never mind; it's safe!" assured the clerk. "Things don't stand still long in this country. They may freeze down, but they don't stick!" And he laughed loudly at his own witticism.

"Seems to have moderated," remarked Mr. Bullard, judging by the brilliant sunlight rather than by his sense of feeling.

"Won't thaw to-day, though," the clerk replied, laughing again. "That's the beauty of our climate; no ups and downs to be all the time catching cold in. We set in pretty snug nearly two months ago, and 'tisn't likely to let up before the middle of April. Healthy, sir? I should think so! Lung trouble unknown. No catarrh, no pneumonia. Dry and clear as a whistle. If there's a climate under the sun that can beat death and the Devil, here you have it. I myself was bordering on consumption when I came here, and now I wouldn't be afraid to fight a prize match with the first pugilist in the country."

The ladies did not get their trunks that day nor the next, lively as things moved in Fargo. But they had not grown to the demands of the city, or of society, so after breakfast they started for a walk in their travelling-dresses. Their cloaks were of heavy wool material, Mrs. Bullard's bordered with fur, with a generous fur collar. Her bonnet was velvet, modern and diminutive. Mira wore a felt hat, stylish and unprotective. They sallied down Broadway. The street was not pretentious by daylight. The best shops plainly showed that half their frontage was false; that is, it was as a very high board fence towering above the single practical story. But often the top of this ornamentation (?) was rounded or pointed into Grecian or Gothic style, truly effective in a certain direction. Time Block was of brick; but the clock's fair face, from which the building derived its name, was only a face. To our party, uninitiated in the demands of the city, saloons seemed unnecessarily numerous. Frequently the angle of a sidewalk contained a shanty of the size and construction of a "switch-house," whose door advertised "Peanuts & Candy."

They afterwards learned that the city encouraged "trade" by granting this use of corners free of cost to any enterprising applicant. These buildings did not tend to enhance the beauty of the city; but it is praiseworthy to foster commerce, and convenient for pedestrians desiring that kind of merchandise. Five times during their walk did the proprietors of thus many different shops rush out upon our party with invitations to purchase.

Before they had traversed the length of Broadway, south from their hotel, Mr. Bullard said he believed 'twas growing cold, and turned up his coat-collar. Shortly Mrs. Bullard remarked that she was afraid they had been cheated in the quality of the cloth from which their cloaks were made, for the cold seemed to penetrate hers as though it were cheese-cloth.

"Aren't you cold, Mira?" she asked.

"Oh, I'm as warm as toast!" that young lady replied; "though the weather isn't quite so mild and springlike as I had expected." Her cheeks glowed with enthusiasm, and her eyes sparkled; but the end of her nose and the tips of her ears were opaque white.

"Je-*ru*-salem!" cried Mr. Bullard. " Your ears and nose are froze, I do believe! I don't know what to do!"

They all paused.

"Oh, dear!" gasped Mrs. Bullard. Mira looked a good deal frightened, but she only said, —

"I don't feel sick!"

"No cause for alarm, Miss," interrupted a gentleman, one of the throng passing in the street. "It is no unusual thing in this climate. I see you are 'tenderfeet,'" he continued, smiling. "Allow me!" and he took up snow, and vigorously rubbed the caked extremities. "You had better step into the hotel," he concluded, indicating by a gesture the Headquarters, near which they were standing, "and wrap up. Parts always more tender after freezing."

With expressions of gratitude our party turned to follow his advice. The kindly stranger detained Mrs. Bullard.

"Madam, I see you are unaware that your nose and cheeks are in the same condition. Fortunately your fur and bonnet ties have saved your ears. However, nothing serious will result from a few frostbites," he added in an assuring tone, as he proceeded to thaw the affected portions by a process similar to that bestowed upon the daughter.

He accompanied them into the hotel, and during the next half-hour learned much of the Bullard history and imparted much of his own. He held legal right to the title " Esq.," but dealt largely in real estate, both in the city and country. He made himself so very agreeable that after his departure Mira said she considered their frostbites just the luckiest thing in the world, for now father would know who to advise with in making investments.

The ladies made other pleasant acquaintances among the people assembled in the hotel parlors while Mr. Bullard, with down-turned ear-laps and up-turned coat collar, went back to the Continental and got all their extra wraps, — veils, neckerchiefs, and shawls. By the time he returned, the frostbitten parts had become very red and swollen, and were not a little painful; so they decided not to continue their walk. But they did not pass a lonely afternoon. Those who had been in the hotel twenty-four hours longer than themselves, by virtue of " old residence " politely called; and the clergymen of the city made it a point to go the rounds of the hotels every day, and gather into their folds sheep of their own denomination or foldless sheep.

"We shouldn't have seen so much company home in a year," said Mira, as they wearily prepared for bed. "What a shame that we can't get at our clothes! and the accident of the morning has made us perfect frights!"

"But almost everybody else is in the same condition." Mrs. Bullard remarked this for her own consolation, as much as for Mira's.

Under the influence of a plentiful supply of Pond's Extract, in another twenty-four hours the inflammation caused by the frost had subsided, and their trunks had been unearthed. Both events happened just at the right moment, Mira said; for Mr. Smith, the gentleman who had relieved their emergency on the morning of their first walk, had asked her to accompany him to the theatre that evening. "Opening night! Immense! Straight from Germany! Equal never heard in the Great Northwest! much less in Boston or New York!"

Mr. Bullard hinted to his wife that Mira was taking up a new acquaintance rather suddenly. But he got no sympathy, so went to the office, and, by cautious and circumlocutional questions, obtained the information that Mr. Smith stood high in the estimation of the community, — "A pushing young man! Worth a hundred thousand to-day, if a cent! Bound to be a millionaire in less than a year!"

The prudent father was satisfied, and Mira fulfilled her engagement. If the operatic company fell short of its advertised merits, our young lady was no critic, and pronounced it most attractive; while opera-glasses, often directed to her face, proved that others besides her escort thought Miss Bullard a surpassing attraction. She was already "known" to Fargo society;

and several young men who had previously fed on her charms at a distance, managed before the evening was over to obtain an introduction.

The blond of Mira's complexion was vivified by the fire of the brunette. Her hair and eyes were dark, but not opaque; they sparkled. Her temperament was a happy combination of the mild and lymphatic, whose result is magnetic. Society would have appreciated her at the East quite as much as West. All their little circle in Blankridge did, as well as Alonzo Peters.

Before the expiration of the week that permitted them their room at the hotel, Mira pronounced their accommodations intolerable, and Mrs. Bullard declared herself "all worn out." Two trunks apiece had been appropriated to the wardrobe of the family; but, in packing, Mrs. Bullard had wisely separated the necessities of winter from spring or summer demands: so only four of these trunks needed to be conveyed to such spot as would render their contents available. They had been placed in the hall, on each side of their door, in tiers of two. Discreetly as their contents were arranged, the article wanted was always sure to be at the bottom of the bottom trunk. The place was rather public for the sorting of garments: but the fact that nearly every door on their floor was guarded in a similar manner, and that its proprietor labored under similar disadvantages, helped the situation; for custom makes fashion, and fashion rules modesty.

Mrs. Bullard thought they had better continue taking their meals at the hotel, it was such a social help; so Mr. Bullard undertook the task of finding lodging-rooms at a convenient distance.

"I ought to have been about it earlier," he said, when Smith informed him that he had no apartments on hand. His friend laughed.

"Before night you'll have a choice of twenty rooms, at least. But they won't stand empty; that isn't the way with our people, — yes or no, up and off."

This statement proved true. Before noon he had had the refusal of fifteen rooms; but his decision required such promptitude that no time for inspection, even, was allowed. The ground floor of Time Block was used for stores, the second for lodgings. He engaged two in this building at a venture. It was near his hotel. He was to pay ten dollars per week for each. He was now paying four and a half dollars a day, individually, at their hotel; but for meals only, the price would be fifteen dollars a week for each. Accustomed to the practice of economy usual among the New England laboring-class, and particularly among farmers, whose profits are small, this expense was appalling to Mrs. Bullard.

"We *must* save *some*where," she hopelessly asserted.

After seeing the size of the rooms engaged, Mira suggested that they get along with one.

"I want some of the experience of pioneer life," she declared. "So far, it has been nothing but luxury —

modified," she added, remembering the inconvenience of living in trunks.

"Save at the tap," quoted Mr. Bullard. All his former experience had served to implant a distaste for cramped quarters. But this method of economy was prevalent in Fargo, and Mrs. Bullard had grown into the spirit of the times. So the ladies prevailed, and, in accordance with their mental progress, commenced spending for dress thrice the amount saved in rent.

If the furnishing of this room was commeasurable with its cost, they continued to live in luxury. For a bed, washstand, lounge, a few chairs, and the drapery necessary to divide the room into compartments, they paid almost as much as had been received for the whole handsome, old-fashioned furniture of their home in Blankridge.

By the advice of Mr. Smith, who now pronounced himself an old friend of the family, and with his assistance, Mr. Bullard had already made several investments which this friend pronounced "capital." He had purchased a large lot on Pacific Avenue; he had bought shares to the amount of one thousand dollars in a company formed since his arrival for establishing iron-works on the northwest side of the city, and had purchased two house-lots in that vicinity; he had also purchased a lot on Eighth Street, and another on Ninth.

A few hours after he paid for his furniture, he sold

the lot on Eighth Street at an advance of one hundred and fifty dollars, and one of those near the prospective iron foundry for fifty more than he gave for it. Mrs. Bullard's peace of mind was restored. If the cost of one week in Fargo was equal to the expense of six months' living in Blankridge, a year's profits from the farm in Blankridge would have hardly equalled the profits of these sales; and the city abounded in such opportunities. Mr. Bullard delayed not an hour to rent an office on Front Street, and put out his sign: —

JONATHAN BULLARD,

REAL ESTATE AGENT.

DEALER IN

CITY PROPERTY, LOTS AND HOUSES.

ALSO

IN FARM LANDS.

Mira felt unbounded pride in this gilded board; for the painter had consulted his own taste in its size and decoration, and it shone as conspicuously as does the dome of the State House in Boston.

"That's the way to catch 'em," declared the artist. "Our people like noble views. Our prairies set the example."

By the contracted pronoun "'em," he signified trade. Thanks to his genius, or the demands of the country, or the ability of the new agent, or to a combination of these superlative qualities, business proved "rushing."

It allowed Mr. Bullard hardly time to eat or sleep. His family might well have complained of neglect, only they were too busy to remember whether they encountered husband and father once a day or once a week. Their mornings in the hotel parlors afforded entertainment as varied and charming as society is capable of introducing. Sometimes a card-party, sometimes music; again a reception, formal or informal; and the varieties of fancy-work there in progress were legion. Each lady seemed to know a new stitch or style; and every other lady was "crazy" to learn it, — Mira in a modified degree, but Mrs. Bullard was rabid. During the afternoon and evening they "received" in their room in Time Block.

Twelve o'clock midnight. A voice from the space behind the curtain, politely denominated Mrs. Bullard's chamber, —

"I am all worn out!"

Responsive voice from the parlor, —

"This is intolerable."

Mr. Bullard enters from the common hall.

"Gone, eh, Mira?" referring to guests.

"O father, close the door, please, quick! *What* an odor of onions!"

"Our neighbors do seem uncommonly fond of them."

"I am sure they fry them for breakfast, boil them for dinner, and roast them for supper, and keep cabbage stewing in a kettle all the time."

Many of the twelve families in Time Block "kept house" in their one room, and their evident partiality for certain vegetables was an annoyance to olfactories nice.

"It isn't the smells that are wearing me out," called Mrs. Bullard from her couch; "it's the situation. Of course Mira must have callers. I want her to see people and young folks; but I *must* have a bedroom. I am growing old — fast, and I miss my sleep. And, pa, I am afraid you'll get into bad habits, being out so late nights."

"Business keeps me out pretty often; but when I can get off, I confess it *is* trying to find the room full of company at eleven and twelve o'clock, or one in the morning. I hate to disturb them, so I hang round in the dark of the entry, or go back to the hotel, and perhaps get pinned there by a customer; so finally I don't get to bed until near morning. Yes, I guess we'd better make a move."

"Strange we hadn't thought of it before!" cried Mira. "I have regretted the inconvenience of circumstances as much as any one, I am sure. But we grow into knowledge so slowly."

As a voice from the shades, again came a voice from beyond the curtain, —

"Moving will be expensive; but we shall save it in clothes, if we keep house."

To the uninitiated, this speech would have been ambiguous. Mrs. Bullard referred to that portion of their clothing which had to be laundered. Not to the washing, exorbitant as were those prices, but to the loss attendant upon the drying thereof. It took from four to six days for clothing to freeze dry in the open air. A blow, if not a blizzard, was sure to come up during the time, and the suspended garments, stiff as glazed paper, would crack and part as though composed of material as frail. Mira did not exaggerate when she pronounced the condition in which their clothing was returned, "perfectly frightful." Shirts minus sleeves, body and skirts separated, drawers dismembered, nightdresses sundered. Sometimes the lost parts escaped to the open prairie, sometimes angles of fences or buildings caught and harbored them. If rescued, they were impartially divided among patrons, regardless of their legitimate belongings. Mrs. Bullard expostulated.

"Can just as well dry them inside, ma'am," was the polite rejoinder, "and in one-tenth of the time. Suit us better; and if there is a firm under the great national flag that is bound to suit its customers, ours is the one."

The following week the clothes came home whole, saffron-colored, and odorous as though steeped in a decoction of garlic and tobacco. Language was incompetent to express Mira's disgust. They changed for a laundry less liberal of promises. The firm failed the same day; and the following, a homogeneous mass of soiled linen was returned, of sizes and shapes most alien to the human form. They changed again, and the results were parallel with their first experience. The next change never returned their "wash." "Skipped," Mr. Bullard learned in response to his inquiries. After again trying steam-drying, Mrs. Bullard directed open-air exposure as more hygienic, if more troublesome. Not that much time was spent in mending. "New times demand new measures," Mira quoted, and basted together such parts as came to hand with a dexterity that the legerdemain profession might envy.

Mrs. Bullard mentioned at the breakfast-table that they desired to rent a cottage and keep house. Within an hour she received a call from Mrs. Black. They had often met in society, but never exchanged visits.

"My dear Mrs. Bullard, I hear you are looking for a house. We are going to vacate ours in a few days. It is *so* cosey and pleasant. A grocer has the first floor, with the exception of my husband's office. *So* convenient, you know, to have the necessaries of life all under one's roof. It is in the wood-yard, and the odor of the fresh lumber is *so* sweet and *so* healthy. *Do* come and see it. All the surroundings are quite select."

The wood-yard was close to the railroad yard; but twistings, turnings, and windings, brought our friends to the spot. The grocery was patent from its outer accumulation of barrels, boxes, and packing-cases, while dogs and loungers as plainly marked the office.

Lace draperies at the upper windows revealed the pleasant home above; but the stairway to this aërial Arcadia was not so evident. The only visible doors led, unmistakably, one into the grocery, the other into the office. They sought direction from the proprietor of the former.

"Oh, handy enough! Trust our folks for that. This way!"

Between the piled rubbish and the sides of the building was a path with one of the requisites of that which leads to life eternal, — it was narrow in the superlative degree. At the extreme rear was a door, not fashioned after that of panelled style, but it effectually closed an aperture designed for entrance, for it stuck very tight. Pails, tubs, jars, kettles, brooms, pans, jugs, mops, in short, all the paraphernalia of kitchen use contended the right of way up the steep and narrow stairs. At the top the little landing showed complications still more curious; but it led direct into — a room whose luxurious furnishing suggested the comfort of Abraham's bosom.

"So near, and yet so far," sighed Mira, the door representing to her mind a gulf as far-separating as was that between Lazarus' refuge and the rich man's place of torment.

Though knowing the mode of entrance was not unusual, our friends thought it impracticable, and decided to look farther. Several cottages that were shortly to be vacated had been recommended, and they spent the remainder of the afternoon in visiting them. "Cosey, cunning, and cluttered," was Mira's comment. Much white lace drapery, and the heaviest of the largest sized plush upholstered goods, composed the furnishing, without regard to the space afforded. Such was the supply of Fargo markets; and the old adage, "One might as well be out of the world as out of fashion," had firm foothold in this city.

At the supper-table Mr. Bullard was informed of their movements.

"No harm done," he replied; "but I bought a lot on Twelfth Street to-day, and have contracted with a builder to have a cottage all ready for occupancy in five days. Two loads of lumber were landed on the ground within twenty minutes after the writings were signed."

"Won't there be danger of dampness?" suggested Mrs. Bullard.

"I spoke of that; but the contractor said Dakota atmosphere precluded the possibility. He is a Western man, and well posted. I guess we're all right. The frame will be completed by to-morrow night; and I shall see that good fires are kept up, though he declared them unnecessary."

Mrs. Bullard sighed for a seal-skin sack. Apart from the demands of the climate, their position in society demanded it. Mr. Bullard would have willingly obliged his wife, and several times the necessary sum for the purchase was laid aside; but within an hour after, some "bargain" would offer that promised great profits, and the appropriation would be otherwise invested. During his hurried meals, or when he came in at night before she was asleep, Mrs. Bullard would gain information of his movements, as follows: —

"Have just traded off Lot No. 16, south, at an advance of $75. Cass has taken Lot No. 8, west, off my hands, by which I cleared just $136. Streeter has borrowed $1,000 of me at 30 per cent. I've taken a mortgage on Johnson's cow at 42 per cent. I hold a mortgage on the best team in the city at 31 per cent. National Bank is paying me 15 per cent. The tax certificates that I hold are bound to pay from 20 to 40 per cent."

She knew he held mortgages on farms, on houses in the city, on several sets of household furniture, on five elegant seal sacks, which she saw every day on the street in company with ladies who were important factors in "best society." Both she and Mira felt all the pride of proprietorship in these latter, and were willing to wait the tide of events. The whole family felt they were fast becoming millionaires. To be sure, some losses occurred. A bank failed, where Mr. Bullard had $5,000 deposited. It was a complete wreck. The driver of "the best team in the city" left his horses in front of a saloon one evening, while he went in to get "something warm." The thermometer stood at forty-three degrees below zero. He stayed so long that the horses broke their fastenings, demolished the hack, and were found in the morning "stark as marble," headed against the railroad bank, high up on Front Street. When the cow was finally attached and sold, Mr. Bullard found there were two mortgages before his; and the furniture he had depended upon to furnish the new cottage was spirited away in the night. A financial loss is of course depressing; but when the next turn of fortune's wheel brings a prize, blanks are forgotten.

Fargo ladies often gave private parties, though the size of the houses necessarily marked the character of the entertainment, or limited the number of guests. "Kettledrums" were popular, for the visitors came and departed in succession. Receptions were popular, for these demanded the same routine. Select teas were very popular among the select few. Nevertheless, were large parties, balls, "full-dress assemblies," many in kind and number. For such purpose the opera-house was rented, or a new building before its occupancy. When a store changed hands, some one philanthropically inclined, managed to save an intervening night for a dance. The different church societies held fairs and festivals, gave dinners and suppers, musicales and card-parties; and every description of entertainment closed with a dance. The Sunday services and funerals did not come precisely under this head, only so far as the costumes of the ladies made them festive; for, verily, but for their surroundings,

one could not tell whether they were dressed for
church or opera. Then there were charitable societies *ad infinitum*, whose chief office seemed to be to
hold meetings; and societies named after every State
in the Union, and every real or conceivable state of
existence. Our friends decided not to patronize these
latter largely, for each involved great expense. But,
in a few weeks, Mira's fingers and thumbs were insuffi-
cient to count the number of which she was a member; and her father and mother were equally involved.
Not that Mr. Bullard went much into society,— he was
too busy buying and selling, — but he promptly paid
his dues, all the same.

Since Mrs. Bullard's residence in Fargo, she had
not been so situated that she could entertain. When
they took possession of the new cottage, she felt that
every law of etiquette and hospitality demanded that
they should give a reception. For such an entertainment at their old home, she and Mira would have prepared the food, and some of Mira's intimate friends have
been invited to assist in waiting upon the table. Such
a thing as hired service would have been considered
unpardonable extravagance and ludicrous ostentation.
Blankridge was ridiculously old-fashioned; and our
friends were not only acclimated to Fargo styles, but
naturalized. The services of a caterer, recently arrived from Chicago, were secured; and at enormous
expense, — to Mr. Bullard, — the caterer imported colored waiters from Minneapolis. Mira declared she

felt herself an insignificant guest in the light of their elegance.

The encomiums bestowed upon this entertainment compensated for its cost. "Incomparably select," was the tamest term used. And so well did the doorkeeper perform his part, that only two people were admitted without reception cards, — one a widow, whose brazen tongue and black heart would have known no hesitancy in applying at the gates of paradise; and the other a reporter for a paper whose politics Mr. Bullard did not indorse.

Fargo servants were chiefly of the Scandinavian race, and as new in the country as was the city of their adoption. Consequently, English was an unknown tongue to them. Mira declared that a girl deaf, dumb, and blind would be as efficient as was their Norwegian "help." The phlegm of northern latitudes pervaded their temperaments. Once, twice, five times in three days did Mrs. Bullard change, and each girl proved more stupid than the former. Invaluable time was consumed in efforts to teach them. It interfered with social duties, with church obligations, with æsthetic privileges.

"This state of things is intolerable!" cried Mira, after a few weeks' experience.

"I am all worn out," sighed Mrs. Bullard.

"What's to hinder a change, then?" suggested Mr. Bullard. "The Headquarters's partnership dissolved early this morning. You know Piper, the junior member, was going to be married in a few days. He had his rooms all ready, three of them. Well, the story goes, some business made it impossible for him to attend the opera last night, so he sent a note of regrets to the lady. She was very indignant, and said if he was going to begin thus early to exercise a husband's tyranny, she would teach him what would be her course. So she accepted an invitation to go with Jones, and flirted desperately with him during the whole performance. Of course Piper heard of it before the evening was half over, threw up everything, settled with his partner, and took the eleven o'clock train this morning for Washington Territory. But lively as were his movements, Jones got ahead of him. He did not want to marry the girl, but of course he'd have to; at least, he thought there was a chance for a suit for "breach of promise" if he stayed behind: so he quietly settled up his affairs, — I bought five lots of him before breakfast, — and he started East an hour earlier than the train that took Piper West. But the joke is, Miss Marsden beat 'em both. She somehow got wind of how things were working, and at nine o'clock walked into DeLucie's dry goods store, dressed in all her best clothes, and, while pretending to trade, made herself so agreeable to the clerk, who had known her for more than a week, and made no secret of his admiration, that he popped the question then and there, and they went straight up to the Methodist minister's, and were married on the spot.

Before night our friends were established at the Headquarters, in the rooms fitted for a bride. If the change brought less care in one direction, it accumulated responsibilities in another. The company at the Sherman House was respectable; at the Continental, select; at the Headquarters, choice. No negligee costumes permitted there, no time for lounging. Every hour, every minute, was occupied. If Mrs. Bullard had previously counted her social triumphs great, she knew them now of little worth. The past paled like Venus before the light of the risen sun.

"What are your engagements for this morning, Mira?" Mrs. Bullard asked her daughter, a few weeks after they were located. "Mrs. Upton says DeLucie has an entirely new line of dress goods in, and we are going to inspect them. I think you had better accompany us. We *must* have something; for, with the utmost ingenuity or skill, I don't believe Oscar Wilde himself could make any more varieties or combinations out of our dresses."

"Yes, I know we are fearfully old-style and shabby," replied Mira. "Perhaps to-morrow I can spare a half-hour, but every moment of to-day is taken. My lesson in ribbon embroidery commences at nine-thirty; at ten-thirty I have engaged to go with Mrs. Yerkes to secure the opera-house for the bazaar, and engage the music, and see Morgan about loaning us decorations, and engage crockery; and then I've got to see the lady that promised to personate a gypsy, and hold her to it, for she's as slippery as an eel, and the character has been advertised, so we must not fail. And I must see a half-dozen others who have promised to fill responsible positions, but will surely disappoint us if we do not refresh their memories every half-hour from now up to the appointed evening."

"Yes, it is a trying feature of Fargo society that people are so, we won't say unreliable, but forgetful. Yesterday afternoon Mrs. Goodman had quite a number of ladies invited to tea. At noon some one sent her a ticket to the *matinée*, so off she went; and they came and — went. She pretends she had invited them for to-day, and is *so* sorry for their mistake. It made quite a little talk for an hour last evening; but, dear me! everybody has forgotten it before now, the parties slighted as well. Let me see! I have three tea-drinkings engaged for this evening; one at four, one at six, and one at eight. And as I shall meet many of the same ladies at each, my dress must be changed between. Can't you help me? For the time will be short."

"I wish I could; I am very sorry. But, as I was saying, at twelve I go to the church to practise a duet with Mr. Bateson for Sunday. At two I have promised to be at home to show Miss Kendal that new crochet stitch. At two-thirty Miss Long comes for me to make calls with her. At four I am due at the rectory to the Ladies' Guild; and at five-thirty I drive out to the county hospital with Miss Long, to carry some papers that have been donated. I am afraid the society gotten up in its behalf hasn't much improved matters. There is a constant change of superintendents."

"I don't belong to it," said Mrs. Bullard.

"I did; but when one of the officers objected to admitting Mrs. Buzzel, who had charge of the inmates at that time, and, as far as I could see, really desired their best good, on the ground that we might want to talk *her* over, it looked to me too much like a *gossip* society, so I left."

"Is that all?" asked Mrs. Bullard, referring to Mira's engagements, as she paused.

The younger lady again opened her note-book, —

"At seven Mr. Boyd calls to settle that uncomfortable affair I told you about. Between eight and nine I must be at the Vermont Society, where I hold an office; and at nine Mr. Weed is coming to be decapitated." Mira's feeble smile ended in a pathetic, "Oh, dear!" that proved her not quite naturalized, or she would have considered the situation cause for congratulation, rather than for a sigh.

The "uncomfortable affair," or, rather, affairs, that engendered this emotion were only two offers of marriage, made, one the day before, the other that morning in church after the duet practice. The entrance of other members of the choir had prevented any response to the latter, and Mira wished to make her refusal kindly; for, though she had known the young man only a week, apparently he was inoffensive, and had meant the highest compliment man can pay to woman. So, amid the rapid talk of the newcomers she could only hastily appoint nine o'clock of that evening for him to call at her home.

The other offer had cost her some thought. He was a widower, said to be of irreproachable business standing, as well as social. His age was not unsuited, and the advantage of wealth was eminently on his side. Mira was only mortal, and for a moment she had hesitated. Brief as was her indecision, it encouraged her suitor not to accept her rejection; so from weariness, she had appointed an hour for another interview.

Private carriages in Fargo were neither many nor marked for beauty or style. But livery stables were plenty, and one of these had recently imported a brougham driven by a man in distinctive livery dress. In common parlance, the ladies were bewitched with it. It was rented by the hour at a most exorbitant price; and, as the demand was great, she who was so fortunate as to secure it, justly felt herself queen of the situation.

Dressed in black silk, relieved by trimmings of crimson *moire antique*, Mrs. Bullard stepped into this carriage at twenty minutes to four on the afternoon following the above recorded conversation, an object of admiration to all masculine spectators and of envy to all feminine. Her reign was to last six hours.

Thirty dollars was the price of her sovereignty. Her pride was gratified, though her Vermont training suffered tremors.

At five-thirty the Headquarters's audience were again favored by the sight of the brougham and its *pro tempore* mistress. She had ten minutes in which to change her dress. "Practice makes perfect." Actresses learn to do it in one-tenth of that time, and Fargo ladies were not slow for want of experience. The second time Mrs. Bullard entered her carriage she was arrayed in dark-green velvet, trimmed with apple-green satin. Between her dress and her carriage she felt her success complete; and this knowledge enabled her to eat and drink at the second tea-table in opposition to the strongest digestive objections. Partaking of the cup that doth mildly intoxicate, tea, and of the beverage that doth mightily inebriate, flattery, — "Your dress is *so* charming!" "Your husband *so* successful!" "Your taste *so* unequalled!" "Your daughter *so* popular!" "Your style *so* unique!" — Mrs. Bullard was beguiled into overstaying her limited time by seven minutes. No law of etiquette would allow her to arrive at the next house where she was due later than seven forty-five. Her brain whirled.

"Driver, get me to the Headquarters in three minutes, and I will give you two dollars extra." The road was rough, but the feat was accomplished. Later, Mrs. Bullard discovered that her dress suffered serious detriment from the treatment consequent upon this speed. But her body knew no ill, for her spirit soared on heights that condescended not to mortal estate. Flushed and eager, she entered her room at twenty minutes to eight. The new combination of purple and lavender that lay upon the bed awaiting occupancy further electrified her. She rang the bell sharply. As flame follows the striking of a match, such was the promptitude of the chore-boy. Before the bell had ceased tinkling her door sprang open.

"Find out if Miss Bullard is in!"

"Yes'm. She's in your parl'r; I jes' let a gen'lem'n in there, 'n I seen her."

"Stay! Don't interrupt! Send a chambermaid instead!" And she tossed him a silver coin.

Presto, change! With the next breath enters Mary. Mrs. Bullard, already struggling with the beautiful complicated combination that was to crown her triumph, —

"Here's a dollar for you, Mary! Now help me into this just as quick as you can! But carefully, for it is already coming apart in two or three places."

Pins readily supplied the place of treacherous thread, and before the driver had swallowed more than one smoking glass of his well-earned fee, and while the wheels of her chariot were still figuratively smoking from the haste of their speed, and the horse literally, Mrs. Bullard was again upon the road.

Oh, the inspiration of success! Oh, the joy of supereminence! Time wasteth, money perisheth; the victor's crown is immortal. At the third tea, Mrs. Bullard kept the brougham waiting ten minutes beyond the appointed hour, for which she paid three dollars extra. At that moment all coin was dross compared with the paradise in which she was moving.

Returned to her room, she found its dimensions cramped, its air stifling. She undressed alone. It took her a long time. The structure of her costume gave way in several new directions, and one or two of the pins that the necessity of the moment had demanded marked the fabric with an unsightly rent. She was glad the present diurnal cycle demanded no further effort. In brief, she experienced a decided reaction. She felt unequal to renewing the contest on the morrow. As she sank upon the bed, unbidden tears watered her pillow. "I am all worn out," she sighed; and her spirit cried for its Vermont home, — for the rest, the peace, that haven only could bestow.

During the recorded conversation of the morning between mother and daughter no time had been lost. Each was making her toilet. Mira dressed in seal-brown wool with plush panels, which she wore throughout the day. It was an innovation to be seen upon the street in the same attire morning and afternoon; but Mira usurped privileges, and obtained them. Hardly another lady in Fargo would have dared the experiment.

At the tea-table she appeared in wine-red silk, with trimmings of cream velvet and lace. The dress suited her rich complexion well. She was magnificent. It was cruelty to the widower. He could not give her up.

"I will build you a house better than anything St. Paul or Minneapolis can boast," he urged. "I own lots in every part of the city. Choose your location. You shall keep any number of servants, and have nothing to do but sit in your chair and rock. You shall have a brougham of your own, and a real nigger driver. Yes, by George! I'll import a nigger. I'll have him here before a week's up. Every woman in Fargo shall envy you. I'll import you dresses from Paris, and buy you diamonds. You shall wear diamonds every day, and, by Jove! your eyes will beat 'em. The new Chicago confectioner shall stay in Fargo, if I keep him here at my own expense, so you can always have fresh candy. I will make a private contract with a California dealer, and you shall have fresh fruit every day, and every kind of goods that Great Britain or the United States ever canned shall be stacked in your store-closet. I own farms, full sections, and I'll deed you anything you say. I will, by Jove!"

Mira's eyes grew in size and brilliancy. His offer was magnanimous, and she told him so.

"I honor your zeal, I admire your enthusiasm," she cried; "but," and her voice sank, "I *love* Vermont."

A knock interrupted. Grateful to fortune for thus speedily terminating the interview, she opened the door. Vain gratitude! It had hardly closed upon her importunate wooer before the newcomer threw himself at her feet.

His hair was dishevelled, his eyes wild, his face, alas! aflame as much with whiskey as with passion.

"I love you to distraction!" he cried. "From the first moment I beheld you I have worshipped you! Say you will be mine, or, by all that is mighty, I will blow my brains out before midnight!"

It occurred to Mira that he had none to dispose of, but she only said, —

"Mr. Gunn, you amaze me! We have never met but twice."

"Once was enough! I tell you I love, *love*, LOVE you!"

She feared his shriek might be overheard.

"Hush! Get up and be reasonable."

"Oh, you calm, cold, Eastern nature! I am of the sunny South, but have lived West long enough to catch inspiration from its ozone. My love is as boundless as its prairies! My passion vies with its cyclones! My heart beats resistless as its blizzards! Say that you return my love, that you will be mine to-morrow — to-morrow morning! I brook no delay beyond to-morrow morning! See! I have bought the ring. It took my last cent — but love is supreme!"

He grasped her hand, and strove to press the golden circlet upon her finger.

"Where is your home?"

"In paradise, for I am beside you."

She held herself calm. "But you board somewhere?"

"I suppose so — on Ninth Street."

"Well, go home now; that is the best place for you."

"Depart from you? Never! Our souls are wedded."

"Mr. Gunn, you must go home now, and give me time to think."

"Think! What about? You have promised to marry me, haven't you? You did promise, didn't you?"

"Go home now; that's a good boy! Promise me you will go straight home, and I will write you a letter."

"Oh, bliss! I obey. But, remember, I shall come for you in the morning, and if you disappoint me, I will blow my brains out."

"Poor boy, away from home and friends!" sighed Mira. "I will try to be a sister to him." She found pen and paper, and wrote him such a letter as she would wish Jonnie to receive were he grown, and exposed to Fargo temptations. Her mantel clock struck eight as she sealed the envelope. She rang the bell.

"Waiter, mail this, and have a carriage at the door in three minutes."

Her orders were obeyed, and at nine minutes past eight she was in her seat at the hall where the Vermont Society held their meetings. Had time permitted, she was conscious she would have felt weak and tremulous; but, remembering that the session lasted only an hour, she held her nerves in check. Obedient to her office, that of secretary, she read the reports. Conversation followed; and as this society prided itself upon its intellectual superiority, the strain to sustain the reputation was tremendous. At nine the meeting adjourned. Her carriage was in attendance, and a half-dozen gentlemen pressed forward, eager to "see her home." But she had long since learned to give them no such advantage. They were "bother" enough without.

The driver of the hack spent the hour Mira was at the Vermont Society in a saloon. The horses passed the time tied to a post outside its door. Opposed as was the temperature of the two places, the effect wrought upon each was the same. The former was frenzied by drink, the latter were unmanageable with cold. To escape escort, she sprang into the carriage, and somehow the driver scrambled to his seat, the horses already in motion. A wild race ensued. Through what streets it took her, or over what distance, Mira never knew. She closed her eyes, though the night was pitchy dark, and clung, breathless, to her seat. Fortunately the man was beyond any attempt to guide the animals, and instinct soon brought them to their stable. It was only ten minutes past nine, but a lifetime of terror had been crowded into that short space. Hostlers were in attendance; but Mira preferred to leave the carriage there, and walk home alone.

The passage to her room led past the hotel office. The clerk detained her.

"Mr. Camp is waiting in your parlor. He said he had an appointment, and I let him in there."

Mira suppressed a groan. "After all, to-day is no worse than all the days." she reflected. "Only sometimes it is one thing, and sometimes another."

Mr. Camp had not made his declaration of love in the calmest manner in the morning, and in the interim his mood had grown even more stormy.

"You have encouraged me," he vehemently affirmed. "You have sung a duet with me in church. You have met me for practice! My manner must have betrayed the volcano in my breast! The passion of my voice meant love for you! Earth will become elysian as we go singing through life together!"

Mira said imagination failed to transport her thither; that his proposal was as undesirable as unexpected.

Then he accused her of coquetry, and threatened punishment dire through exposure. In vain she declared he had never given her any grounds to suspect his sentiments; that, in their few meetings, not even the freedom of friendship had been established.

"I don't know Eastern customs!" he exclaimed; "I am a citizen of the noble West. I carry a pistol and a bowie-knife. You shall be my bride, or the bride of a groom more exacting!" and he emphasized this threat by half drawing from his pocket the boasted knife. Mira shuddered. The features before her were transformed, and in this new light he seemed capable of any desperate deed. She felt herself unable to cope with such a character.

"Be generous!" she cried. "Give me until tomorrow!"

"Until to-morrow, then. But beware!" As he departed he impressed this caution by giving her a glimpse of his revolver.

At the moment Mrs. Bullard crept, sobbing, between her sheets, simultaneously Mira threw herself on her bed in a passionate burst of tears.

"This is unendurable!" her spirit cried. "Why, why, did we ever leave Blankridge?"

Her mental voice found no response, so she wept on, disconsolate.

Mr. Bullard now owned so many town lots, his condition was similar to that of Alexander the Great, who wept that there were no more worlds to conquer. Why not add to the city limits? his brain evolved. Bullard's Addition would sound equally well with Darling's, Tyler's, or Lowell's. Yes, he would purchase land just outside the city, get it incorporated, stake it into lots, then "boom" them. He was well posted in all the current lexicology. Only one little hindrance stood in the way of his scheme. With his present investments he lacked sufficient capital. Of course he could rent money, but here his inherited caution prevailed. While he was still debating the subject, a new arrival in town settled the question, and to his satisfaction. Mr. Hicks would go into partnership — Bullard and Hicks's Addition. Without delay the ground was found, purchased, and all the legal formalities necessary to include it within the city, transacted. The streets were marked to run at right angles, and given sounding names. Cheap, fertile, healthy, aristocratic, electric light, horse-cars, city reservoir, were terms so skilfully mingled in the advertisements, that after a few days the proprietors themselves, as well as the general public, felt that these improvements were an actual present possession, instead of a future possibility.

Several lots were sold. Mr. Bullard was satisfied with their progress, but Mr. Hicks was impatient. He had only run up to Fargo for the winter. In the spring he intended resuming business in St. Paul, and his money would be needed.

"Let's advertise a great sale," he proposed. "Charter trains from the east and west. Send a band up and down the city. Let somebody lead a bear, rhinoceros, or kangaroo. Have a free lunch on the grounds. Make the boys lively by something warming for their insides, and before night we'll have every lot of land off our hands, and be ready to retire with all the business we want, to look after our money."

"I will sleep on the proposition," said Jonathan Bullard.

He was now pretty well versed in real-estate business. He knew all its ins and outs. He had invested in everything as it came to hand, had made piles of money, and had lost more than he originally brought to Fargo. He had never stopped to balance accounts; Western trade has no time for such tedium. The plan proposed by Mr. Hicks held risks. It might prove an overwhelming success, and, without any apparent cause, it might be utter ruin. The expense of advertising, trains for transportation, and the lunch would be enormous. If the "lots" did not sell, it would embarrass them with an unreasoning stigma that time alone could remove. Such had been the fate of whole proposed townships; and again, a like proceeding had been known to make men millionaires in a half-day. No mortal could predict whether they could get a crowd together, or still less whether, being collected, they would purchase. Nevertheless, Mr. Bullard decided he would run the risk as far as the sale was concerned: it was the lunch that deterred him, or, rather, the liquor. He had been brought up on strictly temperance principles. He voted for prohibition, and, unlike most of his business associates, had brought his principles with him when he came West. So he and his partner "split."

"Couldn't sell a damned cent's worth without the drink," the latter insisted. "Sale 'd be as dry as the boys' throats. I tell yer, drink and success go together. Boys will have it. It's no odds whether we give it to 'em, or the saloon-keeper. And they need it, too, in this damn climate."

Mr. Bullard was tempted, and asked another night for consideration.

Rectitude prevailed.

"I'll sell out to you," he announced the next morning.

Mr. Hicks indulged himself in further profanity, but accepted the offer; and before night Bullard's name was stricken from the Addition.

Mr. Hicks carried out his proposed programme. He imported a bear and a monkey; and for a week a man, who bore on his back a placard advertising the sale, exercised these animals throughout the city. They knew no tricks, and looked decidedly forlorn, especially after their keeper had taken his forenoon potation; for then he beat them a good deal, and forgot to give them dinner or supper. But they continued interesting to schoolboys, the poorest and meanest among whom knew enough to know that the monkey was superior to its master; and they hoped that some day, when he had been more abusive than usual, the bear would eat him up.

Three days before the sale, an old chariot, painted in flaming colors, and drawn by four mules, tandem, perambulated the streets, the occupants of the same discoursing music from varied instruments, weird, wild, merry or sad, according to the state of their spirits, influenced by the amount of spirituous indulgence allowed by their finances.

The culminating day, the day of the sale, was the day that saw the height of Mrs. Bullard's triumph, and witnessed the final triumph of her weary flesh; the day that thrice gave Mira a chance to change her maiden estate, and finally saw her wearily crying for home. Every department of business in Fargo was *qui vive* on that day. A free ride was sure to be patronized, — St. Paul, Minneapolis, and all intervening stations from the east; from the west, Bismarck, Jamestown, Valley City, Casselton, including lesser stations. The restaurants, hotels, and saloons alone expected a day of rest. The free lunch would spoil their business.

As was predicted, the trains poured in thousands of people. It was estimated that by ten o'clock in the morning the population of the city had quadrupled. Hicks's spirits were so elate that he moved in aërial space, propelled as is the swallow. Standing in his office door, Mr. Bullard gave up trying to count the strangers. He sympathized with his former partner's exultation, though his muttered, "Couldn't 'a' looked my children in the face otherwise," proved he was satisfied with his own course.

At noon, the hour when lunch was served on Hicks's Addition, not a man could be found on Front Street or Broadway. Thus far was Hicks's Great Sale patronized. The common herd ate his food, and emptied his kegs of beer, rum, gin, or whiskey to the dregs. The professions and city officials ate at a separate table, and made havoc of the bottled drinks. When the auctioneer mounted his stand, jests from every direction assailed him. They would have "squelched" any but a Western man. He stood his ground. Deprived of fun in that direction, the crowd scattered back to the main streets of the city. They were in good-natured mood, — most of them in a mood for trade, though too shrewd to snap at Hicks's bait. Such sharp angling must mean a bogus worm, they said. "Takes a rogue to catch a rogue." The real-estate dealers on Front Street and Broadway reaped the advantage of Hicks's Great Sale. Town lots, town houses, farms, mortgages, bank-stock, changed and exchanged hands. Mr. Bullard came in for his share of bargains. Money rattled in and out of his drawer like dice in their box. He made only cash sales. This was not the crowd to trust beyond the range of vision. If one hadn't the money, another had. As night approached, "the combat thickened." Many lost customers by going to supper. Our friend's stomach made no demand on his brain. He was as independent of food as a god. He was unconscious of volition. Customers came, purchased, and departed with lawyers, who were reaping their share of profits by settling legal formalities. The scratchings of the pens of their clerks pervaded the atmosphere like the hum of steam-sped machinery.

At eight o'clock the specials bore east and west the patrons of Hicks's bounty, if not of his land.

"There goes the whistle!" cried Mr. Bullard to his clerk, as the puff of departing trains reached their ears. "Now we can cool off."

Their brows exuded perspiration that bespoke a raging furnace within.

"Bill, step out and get us an icicle. We've had a pretty warm time of it."

Master and clerk wiped their faces, and held the grateful beverage in their mouths, but Bill uneasily. Presently he spoke, —

"A beefsteak would cool me quicker."

Mr. Bullard laughed. "Thinking of supper, hey? Well, 'tis about time. You've done well. Here's an extra," and he tossed him a ten-dollar-bill. "Don't spend it in drink.

"Hope I've made as much," he meditated, with a sudden thoughtful air, as Bill's flying footsteps echoed down the street. At this moment it occurred to him to take account of stock, — with all his buying and selling, a precaution he had never yet adopted in Fargo. The wheels of his watch sped round. Time neither hastened nor delayed. The hands indicated nine, ten, eleven, and twelve o'clock. The rosy flush of success had gradually fled from Mr. Bullard's cheek. From pale it grew to sallow, and sallow finally gave place to pallor. If his individuality was intact, if this man that seemed to sit in his chair, at his desk, in his office, handling his books and papers, by the light of his kerosene lamp, was Jonathan Bullard, born in Blankridge, Vermont, on the nineteenth day of April, in the year of our Lord 1822, migrated to Fargo, Dakota, on the thirty-first day of December, 1878, this same Jonathan Bullard was dispossessed of every penny's worth of Dakota property, city or country, mortgage or proprietorship: while he held in his hands legal coin, or bank-notes of legal tender, to the amount of 18,637.23, — just $354.31 less than this same Jonathan Bullard took away from Blankridge, Vt., three months before, lacking five days.

"I believe it's all a dream," he muttered. "But, by Jehoshaphat! if I don't wake up five days from to-night and find myself at home, then my name isn't Jonathan Bullard."

He buried his money in his trousers pockets, threw the loose papers on which he had been scribbling into the stove, turned the key to his office for the last time, and with rapid strides sought his hotel.

"Guess 'twill be a tussle with the women-folks," he thought, as he mounted the stairs with a tread that betokened, conquer or die. He did not attempt to open his chamber door softly: for he intended to commence the siege that very night, and to wake Mrs. Bullard by his entrance would be a gain on time. His pleasant surprise to find the lamp burning was merged into wonder when both "his women-folks," in country parlance, rose "on end" in bed. For a moment the two parties viewed each other doubtfully.

"I am all worn out," groaned Mrs. Bullard.

"This is unendurable," moaned Mira.

"Let's go home, then," chuckled Mr. Bullard.

"Oh! will you? will you?" cried the women, springing from "end" to feet.

"Jonathan Bullard, this is no time for fooling."

It was the wife who spoke. She felt that the occasion demanded sincerity.

"I will be ready to start at seven o'clock to-morrow morning," was her husband's rejoinder.

Mrs. Bullard turned to her daughter, —

"Mira?"

"Yes, indeed! We've had to keep almost everything packed for want of closet-room, and what little isn't, we can whisk into the trunks in less than five minutes. Oh, I am *so* thankful!"

"Well, everything's lively in the office yet. I'll go down and settle up, and attend to one or two other little matters while you're about it," responded Mr. Bullard.

The bond between the mother and daughter had always been close, but the events of that evening had cemented it. Mira had not long indulged the luxury of woe in solitude. She sought her mother, and poured all her troubles into that ever-sympathetic ear. Mrs. Bullard confided to her daughter her weariness of their present life, and together they had tried to devise plans by which to induce Mr. Bullard to return home. They had little hope of success, but determined to make a strong appeal, — to entreat, to adjure him to return to Blankridge. The wonder his readiness to leave Fargo would have excited under any other circumstances was now merged in joy. Massed wearing-apparel soon took the place that Mrs. Bullard and Mira had vacated on the bed, and in an incredibly short time that had disappeared within trunks and packing-cases.

"Anywhere else, our going away so sudden would seem strange," remarked Mrs. Bullard, as they stepped aboard the train the following morning.

"Oh, undoubtedly our ears will have a chance to burn for an hour or two," replied Mira. "But I noticed quite a number of passengers got off our train, and the Eastern will bring more. By ten o'clock we shall be as utterly forgotten as though we had never existed."

"We leave under conditions a little peculiar, though," remarked Mr. Bullard. "But they will assist forgetfulness, rather than keep us in mind. I have squared every bill."

PART III

REGRESSION

"HAD anybody told me last year, Jonnie, that you and I was going to be left to do all the spring planning alone, I wouldn't ha' believed them. I never before really felt that I was a poor lone-widder."

Thus spoke Grannie Bullard, sitting with her grandson alone in front of a cheerful wood fire that leaped and sparkled on the hearth of their spacious parlor, as the twilight of April Fool's Day was fast deepening into the gloom of a cloudy night.

"Don't feel bad," replied Jonnie. "You know I am growing bigger every day; and Lon Peters would just chop his head off for you, he is so good."

"Yes, if Lon was your own brother he couldn't be kinder; but I miss Jonathan. I shall never be reconciled to his living in foreign parts. It's been a good while since we got a letter," she continued, after a pause. "I'm a'most worried."

"Oh, don't worry, Grannie! You know they are all awful busy. My! what a pile of money father must have made by this time! No wonder it takes him all the time to take care of it."

"Riches are an awful snare, Jonnie. I am sorry your father's mind is so took up with them."

"Maybe he'll come out all right," comforted the boy with the sapiency of age.

The spring had been unusually cold and drear, so that ploughing was now only just possible. The fields of Northern Vermont could not be ploughed, sowed, and reaped in unfailing routine; they were dependent on the season's temperature. No grain would have time to ripen on those exposed to northern winds at this late planting, so grandmother and son consulted on the practicability of changes.

"I don't have the confidence in myself I used to have," grandmother deplored. "Jonathan's moving to foreign parts has all broke me up."

A rap at the door interrupted her plaint. Alonzo Peters entered. He was a frequent guest, and always welcome. He made things much more cheerful for Jonnie, as well as for the grandmother. They again discussed the spring work at length, and settled to what use each "pasture" should be put. Then the conversation veered to its usual subject, Fargo, and the relation of their family to that city. The evening waned. The late express announced its approach from a distance.

"It's slowing up!" cried Jonnie, his ears alert. "Somebody's come!"

This form of speech indicated that the express-train stopped at Blankridge Station only to drop a passenger or take one aboard; and this was of rare occurrence at the present season of the year.

"I wonder who it can be," said Lon. "I don't believe anybody's leaving town, and I haven't heard as anybody's expected. But there might have been; I haven't been to the store now for two evenings."

Jonnie's thought ran, — "when I'm big enough to do as I've a mind to, catch me staying away two nights!" but his vocal response was, "That's the place to get the news."

"I've been expecting a letter from them for a week," said Grannie. "They've never gone so long before."

"I hope nothing has happened," responded Alonzo; "that Mr. Bullard hasn't been so foolish as to drive out to some of his farms, and they all got lost in a blizzard"—

"And froze to death," finished Grannie. "Such things are common there, Mira writes."

"Father never was risky," said Jonnie.

"No, not till he took to foreign parts," admitted Grannie.

A pause ensued.

"I hear a wagon!" cried Jonnie.

Their house was situated on a road little frequented, particularly in the evening. "I wonder"— but wonder prevented further utterance. The vehicle was certainly approaching at a smart trot, and, wonder of wonders! it drew up at their door. Jonnie rushed out hatless, and Alonzo followed with scarcely less alacrity. Grannie rose, and took a lamp to the window. Its rays fell in direct line upon the faces of the passengers.

"What's up, father?" cried Jonnie, with a face gleaming ghostly out of the darkness.

Lon's tongue was paralyzed, and he felt his limbs equally so. But somehow, he never knew how, he got to the carriage, and put out a hand to assist the occupants in alighting.

"Glad to see you," said Mr. Bullard, heartily wringing the hands of both his friend and his son. Mrs. Bullard kissed each with equal warmth, her wet face leaving its impress on their cheeks. Then came the daughter's turn. Neither knew which made the initiatory move, but Lon and Mira kissed as though their lips would never part. But before this, Grannie had heard the voices, and, simultaneously with the recognition, had set down both herself and the lamp, so they were in shadow. Fortunately, Vermont soil was not conducive to the development of nerves, or the old lady might have suffered from the sudden shock of this return, though the emotion was purely pleasurable.

The maid had gone to bed, but the unusual sound of a carriage had waked her; and she, too, recognized the voices, and jumped up and slipped into her clothes with almost the celerity of Fargo practice. But, quick as she was, Lon was before her in the kitchen, and had the brimming tea-kettle over a brisk fire when she entered.

They all talked, — before supper, while the meal was in progress, and after supper. The conversation was desultory; but the overcharged feelings of each found relief in imparting information, quite as much as in receiving it.

Late as was the hour when they separated, Lon hurried his chores and breakfast to repeat his visit in the morning. He was so early that grandmother and Mr. Bullard were the only members of the family visible. He sought the latter in the barn.

"I don't know what your plans are," he said; "but of course if you want your farm back, it is yours. Somehow, I have felt all the time as if I.was only taking care of it for you to have a little vacation."

Mr. Bullard shook his visitor's hand with a face broadened and aglow with pleasure. He would never have believed Vermont's rugged scenery could make him so glad.

"And what are your plans in case I accept your offer?"

The young man's lips still tingled with Mira's greeting of the night before. It emboldened speech.

"In any case, my plans are — to marry Mira, if she has come back free."

The coveted father-in-law gave a long, low whistle. "Wife used to talk about that before we went away, but I didn't suppose 'twas settled. She's been round a good deal with one and another since we've been gone, but 'twas all the same who with. A girl couldn't live in Fargo, and not get whirled about; but I must say for her, she never got half so flighty as her mother."

"It wasn't settled at all," replied Alonzo, "though Mira knew my wishes before she left. That she has come back, encourages me."

"Well, you have my best wishes for success. She was full as anxious as any of us to get home."

When breakfast was announced, Lon accepted Mr. Bullard's invitation to join them, and he managed to get a seat next Mira.

"I am too excited to settle to any kind of work," she said, as they rose from the table.

"Come out, then," implored Lon. "You ought to see how things are getting on at the barn and about."

"The old speckled hen's got fifteen chickens," cried Jonnie, "and Brindle's calf is just a beauty. Grannie says I may raise it. Come and see."

The girl needed no urging. They went through the barn and its enclosures. Mira was sure the animals all recognized her, and the newcomers recognized relationship. Pattie, the little shepherd maid, would not let go her skirts one moment, and growled with jealousy every time Lon took Mira's hand to assist her in mounting steps or surmounting bars; and he made excuse very often by choosing paths Jonnie's judgment would have shunned.

Then they strayed through the garden. Nature had relented. The sun was on duty, as becomes the sun of April. The south vouchsafed a breeze borrowed from summer. In spite of discouragements, balm and daffadowndilly were peeping little green heads above the soil. Buds were swelling on the lilac bush, and pussy-willows over-hanging the brook hard by had hung out all their tassels.

"Jonnie," called his father, "don't you want to go to Long Meadow with me, and see about ploughing it?"

"You won't mind, will you, if I do?" the boy asked, turning to his sister.

"Not a bit," was her reply; but the next moment she flushed rosy red, for the thought of being left alone with Alonzo recalled their meeting of the night before, and she was not quite sure but she had made the first advance.

"Now let's walk over to your house," Lon pleaded.

"*Yours*, rather." Mira tried to laugh away gathering embarrassment as she turned in the direction of her old home.

"Let it be *ours*, Mira. You have come back; tell me that you come free."

"Alas! I cannot," she whispered.

Alonzo paused, the bright flush on his face turned to pallor.

"I believe" — she stammered — "I think that I didn't go away quite free," and she held out her hand.

Pattie mightily resented the liberty Alonzo took from this confession. She fairly danced around them, barking vociferously, till Lon was fain to desist, lest her turbulence attract spectators.

They visited the other house, the barn, the grounds; and once or twice Mira was beguiled into calling it "ours." The tableau that had first provoked Pattie's anger was so often repeated, that from familiarity or despair, she grew reconciled, and only watched the proceeding from the corners of her eyes.

The express-train had telegraphed an arrival to others than Jonnie on the evening of the Bullards' return, and the "news," in local vernacular, "spread like wildfire:" that is, in the course of a week there was hardly a house in the village that had not heard for whose convenience it had stopped, and discussed the possible whys and wherefores that had brought the family back; and the determination was general to call and find out "for certain." Their return was universally considered a good thing for the town, and curiosity was well impregnated with good-will. But the season was unpropitious for visiting: melting frost made the roads muddy; farm-work pressed; house-cleaning was at hand. Consequently, our Western acclimated friends had time to rest, and settle into routine, and feel a trifle neglected, before visitors arrived. Mira said the days seemed a week long, and Mrs. Bullard had to resort to a nap after dinner to pass away time.

Mr. Justin, the minister, and his wife came first. The Bullard ladies had always been important auxiliaries in church-work, and proved their interest unabated by attending service the first Sunday after their return, though Mira did not resume her place in the choir; and, to the mystification of the whole congregation, Lon Peters sat beside her in Grannie Bullard's pew. This action could have but one significance, and Mrs. Justin gave voice to the general speculation that they must have been engaged before the Bullards went away. Duly seated in the parlor, having first expressed her pleasure in their return, Mrs. Justin said, —

"We should have felt differently about your going had we known how it stood between Alonzo and Mira."

"It wasn't settled until after we came back," Mrs. Bullard confessed.

"They have been almost precipitate, then," commented Mrs. Justin. "It's a serious step."

"Yes, I was afraid it would look sudden to our folks," ·Mrs. Bullard replied; "but after seeing the world, things look different, especially to young people like Mira."

"Alonzo is a promising young man; she might have done worse." Though thoughtful, the minister's tone was commendatory.

"That's just the way I feel," cried the mother. "Why, she had an offer within a week after we got to Fargo, — a real-estate agent; a fine-looking young man, in a prosperous business."

"He must have lacked *character*," said Mrs. Justin severely.

Mrs. Bullard colored.

"Gently, my dear," the husband expostulated.

"But such a hasty proceeding," his wife urged in justification of her severity.

"Oh, not unusual in Fargo!" cried Mrs. Bullard, encouraged by the minister's sympathy. "Why, a young man that had met her only three times came near shooting himself because she wouldn't marry him right away; and a young man that had sung with her only one Sunday in the choir, and met her for rehearsal twice, came near shooting her because she would have nothing to say to him. She had eleven offers while we were gone."

"What desperate characters!" cried Mrs. Justin, aghast. "To think of their being loose in the community, to say nothing of their being permitted in society."

Mrs. Bullard had commenced these confessions with a view to bespeaking leniency for her daughter's present hasty movement, though a little pardonable pride in her popularity had prompted the last announcement.

Though somewhat abashed by the comment elicited, she was not crushed.

"Oh, but the widowers were almost all of them very respectable men!" she cried. "I mean, they were all respectable, though two or three of them did drink rather badly. But every one of them had plenty of money, though father thought some of them rather reckless in their way of conducting business."

Mrs. Justin did not reply to this confidence in words, but every outline of her features expressed volumes.

"Is it true," she presently asked, "that ladies who are looked up to and respected in Fargo society, Christian women, I mean, appear at church in little fancy bonnets made of lace, birds, and flowers? And that they wear satin, velvet, and plush dresses quite common?"

"Yes; I have seen some of our best society there marketing in the morning in dresses just such as you describe. Many of them would consider it almost a disgrace to wear a wool dress on the street; and they go shopping in costumes that in an Eastern city are worn only at a party."

"What a field for a missionary!" and the good woman's cheeks glowed.

"Y-e-s — y-e-s — if one has the moral stamina to stem the tide. But I'll tell you how it is. You fall into fashions without realizing it. The ministers' wives themselves did; and it must have been an awful strain, for none of them got much salary. But, apart from a natural desire to keep up, they had to do it in order to have any influence; for who would countenance a dowdy, were she ever so good?"

Mrs. Justin's natural attitude was erect; she now drew herself *very* erect.

"I should say the dowdiness consisted in unsuitable apparel."

"Well, I must confess you couldn't buy a real good article in Fargo. The stores didn't keep them. The satins *were* sleazy, the velvets cotton-back, and the plushes stiff and coarse. Everything *was* sham."

"How about the underwear?" Mrs. Justin's standard in that line was even more positive.

"Worse still. I had never supposed the country manufactured such rough, coarse cotton goods as that supplied by Fargo markets for winter wear. You could get a tolerable quality of gauze, which was as unsuited to the climate as material could well be."

"So the ministers' wives did not stand firm to their principles?" Mrs. Justin presently asked.

"Well, of course I can't say precisely how they looked at it. Perhaps their principles changed, or perhaps 'twas policy. You know we are told to be 'wise as serpents.'"

Had Mrs. Justin been more lenient, Mrs. Bullard would have found relief in personal confession. As it was, she dared not admit that the substantial wool dresses made for herself and Mira before leaving home had, after a week's acquaintance with Fargo fashions, been stored away in the bottom of a packing trunk, and never again brought to light until shaken out the day after their return to Blankridge; nor would she acknowledge that their wardrobe had been replenished from Fargo's stock of satins, velvets, and plushes, and that reconstruction of these materials had been in constant progress, so that different combinations might suggest a new garment. All this material was a dead loss for Blankridge use; for the mental equilibrium of even the lawyers' wives, who led in fashion, would have been questioned had they appeared in such costume as her trunks contained. And as for their becoming available in the bridal trousseau, Grannie had already pronounced upon such as had been shown to her, — "Not fit for a scarecrow to be seen in."

Mrs. Bullard promised to resume her place in the Dorcas Society and the Temperance League; and in consequence, Mrs. Justin privately commented to her husband that apparently the poor woman was not much hurt (referring to her spiritual condition) by her sojourn in the wild West.

Among Mira's friends the clamor was great that she should come back and take up with a Vermont village beau after all.

"How is it?" "How is it?" she was interrogated on every side. "We thought the poorest and plainest of us could get a husband West, and you was always popular at home. Isn't it true that there is a scarcity of women there?"

"Yes; there has been no exaggeration on that subject, at least. The Episcopal minister's wife told me that she wished to make a party for the young people of their church; and after counting them up, she found the young men numbered thirty-seven, while she could make up only thirteen young ladies, taking in school-girls from twelve to fourteen years of age, at that."

Mira was too modest to state her number of offers, and Mrs. Justin was too conscientious to betray Mrs. Bullard's confidence; but enough facts leaked out to determine several maids of uncertain age to relieve the few young men in Blankridge of any responsibility in their behalf, by testing the Western climate at their earliest ability.

Blankridge tax-gatherers were greatly troubled where to place Mr. Bullard financially. He honestly asserted that he came back "not much worse off either way." But the statement seemed incredible.

"Didn't you go into trade?"

"Oh, yes! Did more work in one day there than in a year at home."

"We can see you have aged; but a man can afford to put a good many years into three months if it makes his fortune."

"And if it don't, he must be satisfied with having bought only experience."

"But how about Mateson? He got rich, didn't he? He certainly paid up his old debts handsomely."

Mr. Bullard smiled. "Yes, he did in Blankridge; but I'm afraid he 'robbed Peter to pay Paul.' He went West within a week after I got to Fargo, — in Dakota, 'West' is nothing short of Washington Territory, — skipped, which means, you know, that he would have been detained had he not left secretly; for his debts were of such a peculiar nature that, loose as is the standard of honor or honesty among the diverse population of a new Western town, he would have had to settle pretty dearly with the law had he been caught."

Public opinion was divided in regard to Mr. Bullard's gains. The "store" congregation suspended judgment. "We'll wait and see how he spreads," they decreed. But he didn't spread at all. Though unaware of curious espionage, when Mrs. Bullard packed away her Fargo finery, she remarked in the privacy of her family, "We've spread enough for one lifetime."

After his betrothment, Alonzo Peters again offered to relinquish the farm. But Grannie saw a Providence in the present arrangement. She declared herself unequal to further active management, and proposed that her son should settle with her. She was very proud of his experience in "foreign parts;" nor could he ever disabuse her of the idea but that it was a great moneyed success, and she advised extravagances of living far more in keeping with Fargo recklessness than Vermont caution. Though not beguiled into ignoring the true state of his finances, this condition of affairs was comforting to Mr. Bullard's self-esteem, and flattering to his pride.

As the whole responsibility of managing his mother's estate had, since his father's death, devolved upon him, and as his son's youth would necessitate his continuance of the care for some years to come, Mr. Bullard readily agreed to his mother's proposition. Next, Grannie proposed a fine new house, with new furnishings. But her son only added two rooms to the old one, saying that the new house should be reserved for Jonnie when he came of age. Mrs. Bullard, Jr., professed herself more than satisfied with the arrangement. In the settlement of Mira, who was married early in June, her heart's desire was gratified. Still, it was evident to her family that she was not quite happy. Wandering attention and long-drawn sighs betokened a mind not at peace with itself.

New England family regard is not demonstrative. Mr. Bullard was aware of his wife's depression, though he gave no expression to his sympathy. "She'll let me know if she wants anything," was his mental comment.

Grannie supposed her pining for Fargo pleasures; but instead of denouncing the sentiment as a weakness, felt pride that her family had enjoyed such delights. On July 4, Mrs. Alonzo Peters proposed to give a family dinner. The invitations included her husband's household as well as her own. The scheme met with Grannie's approval, though she was afraid the attendant labor and responsibility would overtax her granddaughter's strength. Consequently, on the morning in question, she was up before the sun, dressed herself in suitable working attire, folded her best dress smoothly in a carpet-bag, and tied her cap into its appropriate travelling-basket. She breakfasted with her family at six o'clock, and directly after Jonnie walked across the fields with her to carry the dinner costume. He was not to return home; for permission had been given him to go from his sister's to the village green, which promised gunpowder attractions dear to a boy's heart. Presently Mr. Bullard proved them not unattractive to riper years, by "guessing he'd go down and see what they's up to."

Left in sole possession of the house, Mrs. Bullard's mind dwelt undisturbed upon its one disquietude, — her Fargo finery. It lay on her conscience like scorching crime. Until it was clearly off her hands, out of the town, out of the State, she could not be happy. It had no place in a respectable Vermont community. The rich would disdain its sham fabric, the poor deride its flimsy gaud. It was unfit to be pieced into bedquilts, or braided into mats. Were she to bury it under cover of night or solitude, she felt that the earth would refuse to screen her, by casting it up, as it had refused shelter to the tell-tale corpse that Eugene Aram strove to hide. She felt that her packing-box contained a secret as guilty as though its accumulation were the product of a rifled graveyard. Her mental vision saw but one way of relief; and this, thus far, fate had denied her. The spring had brought the usual number of peddlers to other parts of the village, but not one had sought their precinct. She could not solicit their attendance through neighbors, for that would involve questions; and not even to Grannie had she dared display all its folly.

At this juncture of her meditations a loud rap at the kitchen door held the significance of a constable's warrant. With trembling limbs she obeyed the call. Oh, relief! oh, joy! oh, bliss unspeakable! Before her stood a form in mortal guise, bearing upon his head a large tray heaped with decorated glass, colored vases, and plaster-of-paris statuary.

"Exchange for old clothes, marm? Give you a bargain! I've got to be in Boston this afternoon; am leaving on the nine o'clock train. Last chance! Better trade."

Mrs. Bullard required neither solicitation nor advice. The "chance," with its accompanying privacy, had the blessed significance of a dispensation. Heedless of his brigandish aspect, Mrs. Bullard left the man in charge of the lower floor while she sped to the attic. Thrice she made the journey, her arms laden with the spoils of the guilty chest. In all her triumph, her zeal was tempered with discretion. Though she would have gladly given the peddler money to dispossess her of her goods, had it been necessary, she delayed in the selection from his wares, and haggled on prices, until there was only just enough time left for him to reach the railroad station at the hour he had appointed for leaving town. He should have no opportunity to "blab" in Blankridge. In Boston only would her secret be safe, her conscience eased, her victory won.

At nine-thirty Mr. Bullard appeared, punctual to his promise, to walk with his wife across the fields to Mira's.

"Just come from the depot," he explained. "Not many getting on or off the nine-o'clock train. An image man hurried up at the last minute; in fact, he'd have got left if I hadn't motioned the engineer to hold up. He seemed so anxious, I thought 'twould be no use to tell him that I guessed, by waiting over, he could make a trade with you. I shall never wear the old brown overcoat again; and there's a pair of pants that are not worth mending, besides some of Jonnie's out-grown clothes."

"You're a good man! a good man!" cried the happy woman, patting her husband on the shoulder; "but he's been here. I traded off a few old things of mine and Mira's. Yours and Jonnie's are too good. I shall braid them into mats. We need some in the new part."

Her speech was more rapid, her tone higher pitched, and her general manner more excited, than the occasion seemed to demand; nor did Mr. Bullard conceive what kindly office on his part had won her commendation.

Mrs. Bullard had already packed Mira's portion of the purchase in a basket, and they took it to her. It was admired by all, and inspired Mother

Peters with the determination to sort over the wardrobe of her family, preparatory to the peddler's next visit. She stated her intention; but Mrs. Bullard knew that only a patron of Fargo markets would possess stores to exchange for so valuable a collection of bric-a-brac as she had purchased.

Mira received her portion as a gift, and asked no questions. In her present happiness, Fargo experience was remembered only as an amusing dream; and the wedding trousseau had banished all interest in her discarded Fargo gowns.

LEE AND SHEPARD'S POPULAR FICTION

AMANDA M. DOUGLAS' NOVELS

Osborne of Arrochar. By AMANDA M. DOUGLAS. Price, cloth, $1.50; paper, 50 cents.

"In this novel, the author introduces us to an interesting family of girls, who, in default of the appearance of the rightful heir, occupy an old, aristocratic place at Arrochar. Just as it has reached the lowest point of dilapidation, through lack of business capacity on the part of the family, Osborne appears to claim his inheritance, and the interesting problem presents itself of marrying one of the daughters or turning the family out. The author thus gives herself a fair field to display her skill in the painting of character, the management of incident, and the construction of the dialogue. She has been in a large degree successful. We feel that we are dealing with real persons; and, as to the management of the story, it is sufficient praise to say that the interest is cumulative. The book will add to the author's reputation." — *School Journal, N.Y.*

The Heirs of Bradley House. By AMANDA M. DOUGLAS. Price $1.50.

"The author has won a most honorable place in the literary world by the character as well as cleverness of her work. Her books are as clean and fresh and invigorating as a morning in May. If she is not deep or profound, she stirs in the heart of her reader the noblest impulses; and whosoever accomplishes this has not written in vain." — *Chicago Saturday Evening Herald.*

Whom Kathie married. By AMANDA M. DOUGLAS. Price $1.50.

Miss DOUGLAS wrote a series of juvenile stories in which Kathie figured; and in this volume the young lady finds her destiny. The sweetness and purity of her life is reflected in the lives of all about her, and she is admired and beloved by all. The delicacy and grace with which Miss DOUGLAS weaves her story, the nobility of her characters, the absence of everything sensational, all tend to make this book one specially adapted to young girls.

A Woman's Inheritance. By AMANDA M. DOUGLAS. Price $1.50.

"Miss DOUGLAS is widely known as a writer of excellent stories, all of them having a marked family likeness, but all of them bright, fascinating, and thoroughly entertaining. This romance has to do with the fortunes of a young woman whose father, dying, left her with what was supposed to be a large property, but which, under the management of a rascally trustee, was very near being wrecked, and was only saved by the self-denying devotion of one who was strictly under no obligation to exert himself in its behalf. The interest of the story is well sustained to the very close, and the reader will follow the fortunes of the various characters with an absorbed fascination." — *New Bedford Mercury.*

Sydnie Adriance. By AMANDA M. DOUGLAS. Price $1.50.

In this book, the heroine, being suddenly reduced to poverty, refuses an offer of marriage, because she thinks it comes from the condescension of pity rather than from the inspiration of love. She determines to earn her living, becomes a governess, then writes a book, which is successful, and inherits a fortune from a distant relative. Then she marries the man — But let us not tell the story. The author has told it in a charming way.

LEE AND SHEPARD, BOSTON, SEND THEIR COMPLETE CATALOGUE FREE.

LEE AND SHEPARD'S POPULAR FICTION

Home Nook; OR, THE CROWN OF DUTY. By AMANDA M. DOUGLAS. Price $1.50.

"This is an interesting story of home life, not wanting in incident, and written in a forcible and attractive style." — *New York Graphic.*

This volume is larger than most written by Miss DOUGLAS, and contains many interesting scenes and characters. It would be impossible to give a condensed synopsis of the story; but it is enough to say, that it is a fresh, pure, and bright story, full of the touches which reveal intense feeling, and go straight to the heart; but without the overstrained sentiment which was once the bane of novels.

Stephen Dane. By AMANDA M. DOUGLAS. Price $1.50.

This is the story of a mechanic who worked his way up from poverty to affluence. It is complicated by a murder, committed by the hero's drunken father; the victim being the proprietor of the works where both were employed. The hero fell in love with the young daughter of the murdered man, and she became the lode-star which drew him on. Not that she had a fortune; on the contrary, she inherited nothing, and she owed her happiness solely to the exertions and energy of her lover. It is beautifully written, and much admired.

Lost in a Great City. By AMANDA M. DOUGLAS. Price, cloth, $1.50; paper, 50 cents.

"This is the strongest story which has ever come from the pen of Miss DOUGLAS, and starts off with a dramatic touch which chains the reader's attention at once, and holds it closely till the last page is read. It is the story of a little girl, Nora, who, becoming separated from her nurse in the busy and crowded streets of New York, is lost beyond discovery for many a year. . . . The denouement is entirely satisfactory, and the plot of the story is finely conceived and carried out, with not a page's loss of interest on the part of the reader." — *St. Albans Messenger.*

Floyd Grandon's Honor. By AMANDA M. DOUGLAS. Price $1.50.

"The writings of Miss DOUGLAS have found acceptance with the public, because they are characterized by good sense, a keen insight, and an appreciation of all that is good and noble in human life. Her stories are always pure, always pleasing, always elevating. Floyd Grandon is the central figure, around whom are grouped near relatives and friends, together with his own family. The pursuits, pleasures, and lives of this charming circle at Grandon Park make a sunny story whose brightness is not altogether unclouded, for it is shadowed by the villany of Floyd's partner in business, Mr. Wilmarth, whose fate it is not necessary to anticipate." — *Home Journal.*

Hope Mills. By AMANDA M. DOUGLAS. Price $1.50.

This is an entertaining novel. The many characters of the story are drawn with skill, and impress their individuality upon the reader, and the interest is well sustained. But the book is something more than a novel. It was written to exhibit the workings of co-operation in a manufacturing town. Hope Mills, having been closed by a panic and the dishonesty of the manager, are reopened as a joint stock concern by the operatives. The difficulties and final success of the enterprise are portrayed in a lively narrative.

Out of the Wreck; OR, WAS IT WORTH THE VICTORY? By AMANDA M. DOUGLAS. Price, cloth, $1.50.

"This is a strong and fascinating history of a noble woman, fighting her way out of the horrors of a drunkard's home on to the heights of prosperity and peace. Against the mean prejudices of her husband's aristocratic relatives she engages in business, and makes it a success, and this gives her the means of saving and educating her children. It is written with delightful freshness, grace, and strength, and reveals a mind of remarkable refinement and power." — *North Adams Transcript.*

LEE AND SHEPARD, BOSTON, SEND THEIR COMPLETE CATALOGUE FREE.

LEE AND SHEPARD'S POPULAR FICTION

Nelly Kinnard's Kingdom. By AMANDA M. DOUGLAS. Price, cloth, $1.50; paper, 50 cents.

"Nelly Endicott, a bright, lively girl, marries Dr. Kinnard, a widower with two children. On going to her husband's home, she finds installed there a sister of his first wife (Aunt Adelaide, as she is called by the children), who is a vixen, a maker of trouble, and a nuisance of the worst kind. Most young wives would have had such a pest put out of the house, but Nelly endures the petty vexations to which she is subjected, in a manner which shows the beauty and strength of her character. How she surmounted the difficulty, it would not be fair to state." — *New York Evening Mail.*

From Hand to Mouth. By AMANDA M. DOUGLAS. Price $1.50.

"This is a thoroughly good, true, pure, sweet, and touching story. It covers precisely those phases of domestic life which are of the most common experience, and will take many and many of its readers just where they have been themselves. There is trouble in it, and sorrow, and pain, and parting, but the sunset glorifies the clouds of the varied day, and the peace which passes understanding pervades all. For young women whose lives are just opening into wifehood and maternity, we have read nothing better for many a day." — *Literary World.*

A Modern Adam and Eve in a Garden. By AMANDA M. DOUGLAS. Price $1.50.

Bright, amusing, and sensible. A story of two people who set out to win their share of the world's wealth, and how they did it; which, as a critic says, "is rather jolly and out-of-door-y, and ends in a greenhouse," — with some love and pathos, of course, and much practical knowledge.

The Old Woman who lived in a Shoe. By AMANDA M. DOUGLAS. Price $1.50.

This is not a child's story, nor a comic view of household life, — as some might think from its title — but a domestic novel, full of the delights of home, of pure thoughts, and gentle virtues. It has also sufficient complications to keep the thread of interest *drawn*, and to lead the reader on. Among Miss DOUGLAS' many successful books, there is none more beautiful or attractive, or which leaves a more permanent impression.

Claudia. By AMANDA M. DOUGLAS. Price $1.50.

This is a romantic story, with abundant incidents and strong situations. The interest is intense. It concerns two half sisters, whose contrasted character and complicated fortunes are the charm of the book.

Seven Daughters. By AMANDA M. DOUGLAS. Price $1.50.

The "Seven" are daughters of a country clergyman who is not greatly blessed with the good things of the world. The story is related by the eldest, who considers herself far from brilliant or witty, but who makes charming pictures of all who figure in the book. The good minister consents to receive a number of bright boys as pupil-boarders, and the two families make a suggestive counterpoise, with mutual advantage. Destiny came with the coming of the boys, and the story has naturally a happy end.

The Foes of her Household. By AMANDA M. DOUGLAS. Price $1.50.

"This is an exceedingly entertaining book. A simple girl, of beautiful character, marries a young man in poor health out of pure love, and ignorant of the fact that he is rich. His death occurs not very long after the marriage, and the young widow becomes the object of practical persecution by his relatives, who misunderstand her motives entirely. With a nobility of character, as rare as beautiful, she destroys their prejudice, and at last teaches them to love her." — *Central Baptist, St. Louis, Mo.*

LEE AND SHEPARD, BOSTON, SEND THEIR COMPLETE CATALOGUE FREE.

LEE AND SHEPARD'S POPULAR FICTION

LEE AND SHEPARD'S
POPULAR FICTION

J. T. TROWBRIDGE'S NOVELS

Neighbor Jackwood. By J. T. TROWBRIDGE. New Revised Edition, with Autobiographical Chapter and Portrait. Price, $1.50.

"It sparkles with wit, it is liquid with humor, it has the unmistakable touch of nature, and it has a procession of characters like a novel of SCOTT; indeed, in many ways it recalls that great master. There is less description and more action in it than is habitual with SCOTT, and the conception of some of its secondary characters, such as the crazy-brained Edward Longman, would not be unworthy of him." — *John Burroughs.*

Neighbor's Wives. By J. T. TROWBRIDGE. Price, $1.50.

"A new edition of one of the most successful of this favorite author's books. It will be read with fresh interest by many who have welcomed it in earlier editions, and to those who now give it their first reading it will yield delightful entertainment, and unfold lessons that will live long in the memory." — *Gospel Banner.*

Coupon Bonds. By J. T. TROWBRIDGE. Price, cloth, $1.50; paper, 50 cents.

"'Coupon Bonds' is undoubtedly one of the best short stories ever published in this country. It is a most happy and felicitous stroke. It is brimful of the very best quality of humor, — the humor that grows naturally out of the character and the situation, and it moves along briskly, without any urging or pushing by the author. It is full of incident, full of character, full of novel and ludicrous surprises and situations; and, if it could be composed into a three-act comedy, would be as irresistible in its way as SHERIDAN's 'School for Scandal.'" — *Scribner's Monthly.*

Cudjo's Cave. By J. T. TROWBRIDGE. Price, cloth, $1.50; paper, 50 cents.

Mr. TROWBRIDGE's readers are accustomed to plenty of lively incidents and exciting adventures, and in this volume the supply is surely abundant. The story opens with the adventures of a Quaker schoolmaster in Tennessee previous to the opening of the late war, and the exciting scenes attendant upon the opening of the great struggle between North and South are portrayed in a graphic manner. Many of the chapters recall the stories of thrilling adventure that were current in war times.

Three Scouts. By J. T. TROWBRIDGE. Price, cloth, $1.50; paper, 50 cents.

This story is a companion to "Cudjo's Cave" and "The Drummer Boy," in being a narrative of stormy events in the Civil War, when the army of the Cumberland, under Rosecrans, and the Confederate forces, under Bragg, were battling with each other in 1862. Yet it is complete in itself as a story.

LEE AND SHEPARD, BOSTON, SEND THEIR COMPLETE CATALOGUE FREE.

LEE AND SHEPARD'S POPULAR FICTION

The Drummer Boy. By J. T. TROWBRIDGE. Illustrated. Price $1.50.

The author of this book is so famous as a story-writer, that another excellent one is only what all his readers expect. It is a story of the late war, and of a boy who went into the army as a drummer, and who, from the good instructions of a fond and noble mother, sought to impart to his rude and reckless companions some of the good of his own character.

Farnell's Folly. By J. T. TROWBRIDGE. Price $1.50.

All the sterling qualities which have placed Mr. TROWBRIDGE among the foremost of American novelists are to be found in this new romance. It is not a short story or series of sketches that may be "devoured" in an hour, but, as the number of its pages testify, a full-blooded romance, alive with incident, and overflowing with interest.

Martin Merrivale: HIS X MARK. By J. T. TROWBRIDGE. Price $1.50.

This story of New England life abounds in passages of rare humor and pathos. Not even in "Coupon Bonds" nor in "Neighbor Jackwood" has TROWBRIDGE created characters better fitted to give him enduring fame. No one can read the story without seeing that the author has put his whole soul in it. On his last page, he says, and evidently in all sincerity, that he has written it, "not for fame, still less for fortune, but all for love."

OLIVER OPTIC'S NOVELS

Three Millions; OR, THE WAY OF THE WORLD. By WILLIAM T. ADAMS (OLIVER OPTIC). Price, cloth, $1.50; paper, 50 cents.

The book furnishes a most romantic, and, withal, a most instructive illustration of the way of the world in its false estimate of money. All who read the first chapter, entitled "Three Millions," will not be satisfied until they have read the thirty-five chapters, terminating with "The Last of the Three Millions."

Living too Fast. By WILLIAM T. ADAMS (OLIVER OPTIC). Price $1.50.

This is the best novel of a fascinating writer. It is full of incidents of a fast life, and of the expedients to keep up appearances, resulting in crime, remorse, and the evil opinion of all good men. The narrative is replete with startling situations, temptations, and all the elements of a thrilling story.

In Doors and Out. By WILLIAM T. ADAMS (OLIVER OPTIC). Price $1.50.

This volume contains about thirty bright and interesting stories of domestic life, directed against the follies and foibles of the age. They are written in a kindly, genial style, and with a sincere purpose to promote happiness, good feeling, and right dealing in domestic, business, and social relations.

LEE AND SHEPARD, BOSTON, SEND THEIR COMPLETE CATALOGUE FREE.

LEE AND SHEPARD'S POPULAR FICTION

VIRGINIA F. TOWNSEND'S BOOKS

A Boston Girl's Ambition. By VIRGINIA F. TOWNSEND. Price $1.50.

"This is a grand story, grandly told. The little mists which went to make up the shadows of the years in the lives of two young people, the sufferings and privations of Dorrice and Carryl, their struggle upward, and the happiness which smiled upon them at the end of the struggle, will cause the story to linger long in the minds and hearts of its readers." — *Washington Chronicle.*

That Queer Girl. By VIRGINIA F. TOWNSEND. Price $1.50.

The "Queer Girl" is a charming character, and so is Rowan, the real hero. She is "queer" only in being unconventional, brave, and frank, — "an old-fashioned girl." The girls who follow her history, and that of her pleasant companions, are sure of being delightfully entertained; and they may, if they will, take a lesson from brave, unselfish Madeline.

Daryll Gap. By VIRGINIA F. TOWNSEND. Price $1.50.

The celebrity of VIRGINIA F. TOWNSEND as an authoress, her brilliant descriptive powers, and pure, vigorous imagination, will insure a hearty welcome for the above-entitled volume, written in the writer's happiest vein.

"A story of the petroleum days, and of a family who struck oil. Her plots are well arranged, and her characters are clearly and strongly drawn." — *Pittsburg Recorder.*

Lenox Dare. By VIRGINIA F. TOWNSEND. Price $1.50.

A story of New England people, and of life associated with Hampton Beach and its vicinity. The plot is natural and well treated, and the sentiments pure. The story is very entertaining, and, to the thoughtful reader, instructive and stimulating.

A Woman's Word, and how she kept it. By VIRGINIA F. TOWNSEND. Price $1.50.

"This is a thoroughly charming story, natural, wholesome, and extremely interesting. The heroine is a delightful creation, and all the *dramatis personæ* are remarkably well drawn. It is pleasant to come across a novel so entirely worthy of praise, and we commend it without reserve to all our readers." — *Charleston News.*

Mostly Marjorie Day. By VIRGINIA F. TOWNSEND. Price, cloth, $1.50; paper, 50 cents.

In this book, there is the endeavor of a noble and lovable girl to escape from the conventionalities which fettered her life, and engage in some serious duty. She became a nurse, and, in the end, had her exceeding great reward. It is a bright, spirited, and sometimes delicately humorous story, with a well managed plot, and life-like characters.

But a Philistine. By VIRGINIA F. TOWNSEND. Price $1.50.

One of the most pleasing works of this author. It is a story of natural thoughts rather than events; and it is the author's unique coupling of passive subject and vigorous style that gives the work its attractive quality. The characters are strong, and several of the scenic descriptions have the true ring of poetic appreciation, while in conversational passages the diction is bright, pleasing, and varied.

LEE AND SHEPARD, BOSTON, SEND THEIR COMPLETE CATALOGUE FREE.

www.ingramcontent.com/pod-product-compliance
Lightning Source LLC
Chambersburg PA
CBHW021948160426
43195CB00011B/1266